BY WHAT POWER

The Book of Acts, Autocracy, and the Power of Resistance

ERIC C. SMITH

chalice
PRESS

Print: 9780827203563

EPUB: 9780827203570

EPDF: 9780827203587

ChalicePress.com

Printed in the United States of America.

Contents

For Jessa, in our 28th year

Acknowledgements

I am grateful to the faculty and Board of Trustees of the Iliff School of Theology for recommending and granting the sabbatical that made this book possible, as well as to Dean Cathie Kelsey for her guidance and assistance in that process. I am likewise grateful to First Plymouth Congregational Church for giving me time away to complete this manuscript.

A number of people contributed to the cost of a writing retreat at which I wrote the bulk of this book. For their generous support, I thank Grover Wrenn, Emily Bruno, David Menees, Wanda Coleman, Betty Arca, Chris Furr, Hollie Woodruff, Jennifer Loh, Meghan Tschanz, Melissa St. Clair, Ruth Neil, Kelly Matteson, Donna Cole, Boyung Lee, Richie Sanchez, Jason Shelton, Cheryl Breiner, Wayne Coppins, Scott Hardin-Nieri, Ashley Crowder Stanley, Sharon Decker, Pamela Schmidt, Nancy Lindsey, Nicole Nicholas, Heather Godsey, Xyaire Woods, Marcee Binder, Katherine Daniels, Craig Cranston, Kenneth Hoagland, Kelly Decker, Jana Everett, Heidi Stevenson, Roger Meier, Barbara Dendy, and five anonymous donors.

As ever, Hazel, Harley, Eden, and Jessa make everything possible, and my gratitude to them will never diminish.

Introduction

The Book of Acts

The first time I heard of a book called the Acts of the Apostles, I was maybe eight years old and in the basement fellowship hall of the large Southern Baptist church across the street from my house. It was probably a Wednesday night, though it might have been a Sunday afternoon—I went to church a lot. That day I had gathered there with several dozen kids and a few teachers to share some snacks and small paper cups full of lemonade. As we finished the snacks, one of the teachers got our attention and began to teach us a song. "*Matthew, Mark, Luke and John, Acts and letters to the Romans, First and Second Corinthians, Galatians, and Ephesians*," we began, in a lilting singsong tune. The lyrics stretched on for the entirety of the New Testament, right to Revelation, and at some point I learned the whole thing—though these days I struggle to remember how the tune goes at the end. The idea behind the song was to teach us the order of the books of the New Testament so that we could know how to look them up in our Bibles. It worked: today, as a Bible scholar with a PhD and a tenured job as a professor, I still sometimes sing that childhood tune in my head to find my place among the plentiful thin pages of the New Testament.

That was how I first learned *of* the Acts of the Apostles, or the Book of Acts, but I didn't learn much *about* it. That's because just as in the song, Acts in the real world is sandwiched between two big and important groups of books and it's easy to lose track of it. The gospels (Matthew, Mark, Luke, and John) are famous and widely studied. Paul's letters get a lot of attention too, especially among the Baptists in that fellowship hall and the other Protestant Christians around whom I grew up. Paul and the gospels were central in the kinds of religion I experienced as a child, but Acts only showed up every once in a while. We learned a story or two from it—the story of Pentecost from the second chapter I remember, and the story of Ananias and Sapphira in chapter 5. But most of the book remained a mystery to me until I was an adult and began to study the Bible academically.

That's too bad, because it turns out that the Book of Acts is a fascinating and engaging book that is unique among the works of the New Testament. Acts' story picks up where the gospels leave off, in the aftermath of Jesus' crucifixion and death, and it accompanies Jesus' followers from Jerusalem into the wider Mediterranean world, from Syria to Asia Minor to Greece and finally to Italy and Rome, where Acts ends. As Jesus puts it in 1:8, Acts is the story of the apostles carrying a message "to the ends of the earth"—at least as far as Mediterranean people understood the earth and its ends in those days. Along the way, Acts tells many wild and entertaining tales. There are mobs and shipwrecks, serpents and soothsayers, dramatic showdowns and secret escapes. More than any other book of the New Testament, Acts builds a world, fills it with inhabitants, and gives them interesting things to do. Acts would be a compelling book in any context, but within the Bible—which, let's face it, is not always known for its thrilling prose—Acts stands out as one of the most interesting and exciting texts of all.

One reason Acts is so engaging is that it is set against the backdrop of the broader Roman world. This is a little bit rare within the New Testament. The gospels focus mostly on Galilee and Judea, and Paul's letters—while sent to far-flung places—don't really spend much time telling about the particularities of Corinth or Galatia or Thessalonica. Other books of the New Testament aren't much better. But Acts is a book about travel, and it moves quickly from one place to another, traversing large stretches of land and sea. It's a book about place and about people, and—perhaps most of all—it's a book about *power*. Because Acts moves in and through the Roman Mediterranean, it always has one eye on power and power's deputies: violence, division, coercion, imprisonment, intimidation, status, territory, and money, to name a few. From start to finish, Acts is structured as a series of conflicts between Jesus' followers and various forms of power and authority. That makes for very good storytelling. It also makes Acts a very useful book to read in our own time and place.

I'm writing this book about a year into Donald Trump's second presidential term. Whether you voted for Trump or not, whether you like or support him or not, we might all be able to agree that we are living in a time when things are changing quickly. Many old certainties and institutions are passing away and new and unknown realities arriving, for better or for worse. We might also be able to agree that we live in a time of intense debate and discussion about the proper role and function of government. I have heard people from across the political spectrum complain bitterly about the demands and actions of government, and I have heard those same people celebrate when other things were done by that same government.

I don't know about you, but for most of my life I had a fairly predictable and stable relationship with political power. I knew more or less what to expect, regardless of who had been elected. But these days I wake up nearly every day to a news alert that something I once thought was stable and permanent—some law, Supreme Court precedent, federal agency, norm, enforcement priority, or wing of the White House—has changed or disappeared completely. Donald Trump's two presidential terms have left me hyper-aware of the United States government in a way I was not before.

These years have made me think differently about power. They have left me with a new and raw awareness of how governmental power can be used against people by fiat, regardless of what the rules say and regardless of what most people want, and used in a way that I really saw only in history books before. That's not to say I was naïve until now. For my whole adult life, I have held a critical and suspicious view of many of my country's actions. But over the past decade or so, something has shifted. Perhaps you feel that way too.

The central claim of this book is that the Book of Acts—a twenty-century-old collection of stories about how a group of Jesus' followers emerged into the world—can tell us something about our own time, place, and experiences. Now, I don't want to overstate this claim. Our situation is *not the same* as the situation Paul or Peter faced, nor an unnamed Ethiopian court official, an enslaved girl with a gift of prophecy, or any of the other characters who fill the pages of Acts. And I will have more to say below about the dangers of thinking anachronistically or out of step with the period in which we find ourselves now. But now that we're living in a time of argument and conflict about the size and shape and role of government and its power, now that we're aware of how precarious it feels to bump up against the violence and ambivalence and apathy of state power, now that we know for ourselves or through someone close to us how it feels to be on the wrong side of some arbitrary line or to be singled out because of who we are, because of all of this I do think that we now have something to learn from one of the Bible's most sustained descriptions of life under empire. We can, I suggest, take some lessons from the Book of Acts and see parts of our world in its world, recognizing ourselves in some of its stories.

But first we need to talk a little bit more about Acts itself.

What Is Acts?

Acts stands alone in the New Testament; it is the only book of its kind. While there are four gospels and you can't even count all the epistles on two hands, Acts stands alone as the only one of … *whatever it is*. What is Acts, anyway?

Some people call Acts a "history," which is a decent description. Acts does narrate things that happened over time, which is more or less what a history does. But "history" is an imperfect and incomplete category for what Acts is. For starters, ancient and modern ideas about history are not the same. Today we think of history as founded on facts. We associate history with objectivity and a straightforward documentation of the past, even if that's never fully true of any work of history. We think this way because we live on this side of a major intellectual movement called the Enlightenment, which flourished in the eighteenth century and which has influenced our ideas about reason and rationality, whether we know it or not. The Enlightenment led us to associate truth with factuality and to think of history as an objective undertaking. That Enlightenment perspective probably has made us think of history as more objective than it's possible for history to be, if we're being honest.

But if the Book of Acts is a history (which is debatable), it is certainly not a *modern* history. Neither the writer of Acts nor of any other ancient book was aware of Enlightenment-era ideas about objectivity and factuality, and the authors of those works were not interested in those things in the ways we are. The author of Acts, like those of most historical books of its time, was more interested in telling a good story—a *true* story, ancient authors would have insisted—than it was interested in factuality. To take one example that will come up later in this book, Acts is famous for the long and polished speeches of its characters. Biblical scholars have long recognized that these speeches are not transcripts of historical speeches but set-pieces composed after the fact by the author of Acts to capture *what* someone like the speech-giver *should have said* in that kind of a moment.

Reading that might make you nervous. *Is this guy really saying there is made-up stuff in the Bible?* Yes and no. I'm saying—as many New Testament scholars do—that Acts is not a history book in the modern sense, but that it is engaged in storytelling that makes the most of its scenes and characters to convince its readers of certain things. Acts is not trying to be neutral or objective, and its storytelling reflects that reality. The speeches that Acts has its characters deliver always point toward that end—convincing the reader of something. To the author of Acts, getting the style and force of a speech correct was more important than nailing the historical accuracy—and historical accuracy was a tricky thing anyway, in a time before recording technologies or even widespread literacy.

That brings us to some other possible categories in which we might put Acts. Is Acts a biography—a biography of the church? Or is Acts an apologetic work—a book meant to convince its readers of the truth of the Jesus Movement?

(Many scholars call the earliest phase of Christianity the "Jesus Movement" to distinguish it from the later and more fully developed Christianity, so I will often use that phrase in this book.) Or perhaps Acts is something like a novella, a saga, or a travelogue? There is truth in all those categories, just as there is truth in the idea that Acts is a kind of history. Ultimately, Acts defies any easy categorization, and it is the only book of its kind in the New Testament. (There are other early Christian *Acts* that are not in the New Testament, like the *Acts of Peter*, the *Acts of Paul*, the *Acts of Paul and Thecla*, and the *Acts of Andrew*, among others. Like the Acts of the Apostles, these books make for very interesting reading.)

We might be better off if we give up saying what Acts *is* and instead focus on what Acts *does*. What Acts *does* is situate a religious story and a collection of theological claims within a sweeping narrative set against a dizzyingly widening world. Acts takes its readers on a journey, but it's a journey with a purpose. It's a history, but it's a history meant to convince us of something. Acts follows its characters as they pass across space and time. And—*this is important*—Acts follows the story of Jesus' first followers as they leave the easternmost edge of the Roman Empire and move west across the empire's vast territories, until the story finally comes to a rest in the city of Rome itself. In the end, *Acts tells the story of Jesus' first followers with a vocabulary and a grammar of power, violence, and territory.*

To understand why it tells the story that way, let's turn to the questions of who might have written Acts, when, and for what purpose.

Who Wrote Acts, and When, and Why?

The Book of Acts is anonymous. The simple truth is that we don't know who wrote it, and whoever *did* write it didn't think that detail was sufficiently important to include it anywhere in the book. But in spite of that fundamental limitation, there are some things we can say about the person who wrote Acts.

Like any author, the person who wrote Acts left clues. A few of these clues help flesh out the author in a general way, but they don't bring us close to anything specific. For example, the author of Acts writes in pretty good Greek—not top-notch, literary Greek, but definitely proficient. And the person who wrote Acts seems to have had a fairly worldly profile. They seem to have had detailed knowledge of a wide swath of the Mediterranean, and they got the geography and local customs more or less correct. (Scholars have noted that the author of Acts seems to have had especially accurate information about some of the Greek cities like Corinth and Thessalonica.) So we begin to get a picture of the author as an educated person who has traveled enough to know about life in a variety of places throughout the Roman Empire, perhaps especially Greece—someone well-suited to writing a book like Acts.

The largest clue to the identity of the author of Acts is that they probably also wrote the Gospel of Luke. That's why many books about Acts refer to the author as "Luke." Don't get too excited, though: the same thing that's true of Acts is also true of all four gospels. The gospels are all anonymous too, and the names attached to them (Matthew, Mark, Luke, and John) are part of an old tradition, but the names aren't part of the gospel texts themselves. So knowing that "Luke" probably wrote Acts doesn't necessarily get us any closer to figuring out anything specific about who "Luke" was. Still, it's exciting to be able to recognize that a single author was probably responsible for both Luke and Acts. Many scholars even call the books Luke-Acts, treating them as a single multivolume unit, or as so closely associated with each other that they can be studied and analyzed together.

Why do scholars think the same person wrote both Luke and Acts? There are several very good reasons.

The first is that the two books share a lot of distinctive vocabulary and grammatical quirks, and just as you can probably spot the prose of your favorite author because of their word choice and sentence structure, so we can recognize the ways Luke and Acts share some linguistic characteristics and we can surmise that they were written by the same person.

Second, the books share a lot of themes. For instance, many scholars have argued that both books show more awareness of and interest in women than the rest of the New Testament, and they both have a lot to say about how the lowly people of the world—the overlooked, the downtrodden, the neglected—are actually the ones to whom God pays the most attention and whom God favors. Justo González is a good example of this scholarly perspective.[1]

Third, if you look at the opening lines of both books, you'll see that Luke and Acts both include a reference to the writing of the books themselves and a mention of a person named Theophilus. This turns out to be important because it tells us that the author of Acts (whom we will call "Luke" with masculine pronouns because it's easier than saying "the author of Acts" every time, even though we don't actually know the author's name or gender for certain) was thinking carefully and self-consciously about the task of authoring a book, in the way a historian might. It also tells us that Luke probably had a patron or at least a specific audience in mind—a man named Theophilus for whom

---

[1] Justo L. González, *The Story Luke Tells: Luke's Unique Witness to the Gospel* (William B. Eerdmans, 2015).

Luke was writing and who presumably would be receiving copies of both the Gospel of Luke and Acts.

But that's not all.

In Luke 1:3, right at the beginning of the book where the author is addressing Theophilus directly, he calls him by a specific Greek word that is usually translated "most excellent." In English this sounds like a really enthusiastic way to refer to someone. There's actually more than just excitement behind these words. The Greek word Luke uses there was commonly used to refer to someone with a position in the Roman governmental hierarchy. And—here's the kicker—the *other* three times that Greek word appears in the text of Luke-Acts (which all come in chapters 23–26 of Acts), that word either refers directly to a representative of the Roman Empire or is used in the presence of one of the empire's representatives. So it seems to be a word that Luke reserves for situations of addressing Roman officials. That makes many scholars certain that Theophilus—Luke's addressee—was himself a Roman official.

So what? Well, that little detail turns out to be important. If Luke is writing Acts with a Roman official in mind, knowing that someone with a position in the government is going to be reading his words, then a lot of his stories take on additional meaning. As we will see, Acts returns to scenes of Roman power almost obsessively, again and again putting the characters of the book into scenes where they engage with Roman officials, usually on very unequal terms. Those Roman officials, for their parts, often turn out to be corrupt, incompetent, feckless, or disinterested. It's not a very flattering portrayal of the empire's strength and efficiency. That makes sense, if you think about it; this is the same Roman Empire that, on flimsy charges, unjustly executed Jesus in Luke's first volume, murdering him on a cross. It might not be surprising that Luke has a low opinion of such officials' effectiveness. But it *is* surprising, I think, that Luke is putting all of this in a book that he knows will be seen by someone with a position within the empire itself. Maybe Theophilus was sympathetic to the Jesus Movement and Luke knew that and wasn't worried about reprisals. Or maybe Theophilus commissioned the books we know as Luke and Acts precisely so that he could get an insider's view of the Jesus Movement and some unfortunate episodes in Roman administration. We will never know.

In a larger sense, we will never know why, exactly, Acts was written. It might have been that Theophilus commissioned the book and Luke obliged his patron's interest. It might have been that Luke simply thought it was an interesting story worth telling. But Luke gives us an important clue in his Gospel, in the first verses of the whole book:

> Since many have undertaken to compile a narrative about the events that have been fulfilled among us, just as they were handed on to us by those who from the beginning were eyewitnesses and servants of the word, I too decided, as one having a grasp of everything from the start, to write a well-ordered account for you, most excellent Theophilus, so that you may have a firm grasp of the words in which you have been instructed. (Luke 1:1–4)

This introduction to the Gospel of Luke tells us that Luke was thinking about the need for a "well-ordered account" of the followers of Jesus and the way the Jesus Movement emerged into the world. There's a little bit of criticism built into Luke's words here; he seems to imply that *other* accounts were not as orderly as he would have liked. If a satisfactory account had existed, there would have been no need for Luke to write another.

And again, the question of Theophilus' identity hovers above all of this. If Theophilus was an official within the Roman governmental hierarchy, then the "well-ordered account" might have been a way for Luke to explain some of the Jesus Movement's characteristics to someone in power. The movement, after all, faced some accusations and prejudices in the popular imagination. Its leader had been crucified as a criminal, and many of its most prominent figures had similarly run into trouble with the law. And, in a world where most people understood the world to be populated with multiple divinities and the Roman imperial apparatus thought that pleasing the gods was key to maintaining a good social and political order, the followers of Jesus stuck out like a sore thumb. For they claimed that there was only one God, not many, and moreover they claimed that a Judean peasant was the son of that one God. In short, Jesus' followers were *weird*. There were a lot of rumors and speculation flying around about the Jesus Movement, so perhaps the best thing we can say about why Luke wrote Acts is that he wanted to set the record straight. A "well-ordered account" was a good way to expose people—especially powerful people like Theophilus—to the movement's ideas and stories. A good book, Luke understood, was a good public relations exercise.

That brings us to a final question about the composition of Acts: When was it written? (And why does it matter?) Scholars are divided on the first question. Some think Acts was written relatively early in the history of the Jesus Movement, perhaps even in the 70s, just a few years after the Gospel of Luke was written. That would line up with the narrative of Acts in certain ways. The Book of Acts ends with Paul imprisoned in the city of Rome, which would have happened sometime in the late 50s or early 60s. But Acts doesn't tell us what happened to Paul after that; it doesn't say whether he was released, executed, or something else. So it might make some sense to say that Acts was written at a moment when Paul's fate remained unknown. The idea that Acts was written relatively early, perhaps in the 70s, also helps when we try to imagine the relationship between Luke and Theophilus staying essentially the same between the Gospel and Acts. If only a few years had passed, then it makes sense that the client-patron relationship between the two would have remained unchanged.

But other scholars, especially more recently, have pushed for later dates. A range between the years 80 and 100 is perhaps the most common scholarly consensus these days—soon enough after the Gospel of Luke and the events described in Acts that Luke and Acts could function as a two-volume set, but late enough that some of the traditions and stories about figures like Peter and Paul had had time to circulate and solidify. Some scholars see evidence that Acts knew about, and made use of, the books of a historian named Josephus, who wrote his major works from the mid-70s to the mid-90s. If those scholars are correct, then it's hard to imagine Acts being written in the 70s, and a date in the 80s or 90s becomes more probable. Some modern-day scholars, most notably a consortium calling itself the Acts Seminar, have concluded that Acts must have been written in the early second century, perhaps around 110 or 115.[2] The problem with that perspective is that the author of the Gospel of Luke would have aged, and it would be less likely that both Luke and his patron Theophilus would still have been alive by the early second century.

As you will have noticed, there are problems with all these hypotheses about the date of Acts. Splitting the difference, most introductions and textbooks will typically give a date of 80 to 90 C.E.

Why does any of this date stuff matter? And what does all that information tell us about Acts as a book and how we should interpret it? It helps us to get a sense of when Acts was written, by whom and for whom, and why. Knowing how and when Acts entered the world helps us get a sense of how we should interpret it, and especially how we should understand its many references to Roman imperial governance, power, violence, and territory.

The first takeaway is that no matter which date we accept for the composition of Acts, the book was written at the height of Roman imperial power, from somewhere within the Roman Empire, and likely with an audience that included someone (Theophilus) within the Roman governmental structure. Acts was written in the decades during which the autocratic power of the emperors had become fully entrenched and power was firmly in the hands of

[2] Dennis E. Smith and Joseph B. Tyson, eds., *Acts and Christian Beginnings: The Acts Seminar Report* (Polebridge Press, 2013).

a series of rulers called Caesars. Acts was written about, and for, a world of autocratic rule. Rome itself was an empire, which means it controlled large chunks of territory from a smaller center. In the case of Rome in the first and second centuries, imperial governance was centered in the city of Rome, but from there it controlled territories as far west as Spain, as far east as Judea and Syria, as far south as North Africa, and as far north as northern modern-day England. In fact, it was during the reign of an emperor around the time Acts was written—Trajan, who ruled from 98 to 117—that the Roman Empire reached its maximum size. A network of provincial officials, military officers, and client rulers helped keep the empire running—usually (but not always) smoothly. Acts introduces us to many of those officials, officers, and rulers.

The second takeaway is that Acts was written in the aftermath of one of the times in which Roman governance was running a little less smoothly, at least in the east. From 66 to 70, one of Rome's easternmost provinces, Judea, rebelled against the empire. Judea was the province in which Jerusalem was located, and it's where many of the stories in the gospels and Acts take place. This conflict is known as the First Jewish War (because there was another rebellion of diaspora Judeans from 116 to 118, sometimes called the Second Jewish War, and a huge rebellion from 132 to 136 called the Bar Kokhba Revolt) or sometimes either the Second Jewish War *or* the Third Jewish War, depending on whether you count the one from 116 to 118. Suffice it to say that the province of Judea gained a reputation as a troublesome part of the empire, and anything associated with Judea was probably viewed with suspicion. Jesus was executed by the empire in the province of Judea as a political rebel a few decades before the outbreak of the First Jewish War, so *both* the followers of Jesus whose stories are found in Acts *and* the Jesus Movement itself probably faced a bit of an uphill battle against public opinion. That might well be part of the reason Luke wrote Acts for Theophilus in the first place—to demonstrate that the followers of Jesus were not rabble-rousers, criminals, and instigators of chaos, but that instead they were harmless, pious people who had been treated unfairly by Roman authorities. That possibility will become important later in this book, as it helps us to understand why Acts spends so much time talking about the inefficiency, unfairness, and capriciousness of Roman authority. Acts lingers on moments when Roman imperial power acted unfairly because part of its story is about how the Roman Empire misunderstood Jesus and his followers from the beginning.

The third takeaway from all this information about when, why, and by whom Acts was written is related to the second—namely that Acts was written at a time when the Jesus Movement was gaining traction throughout the

Roman Empire and gaining attention, too, not all of it positive. Followers of Jesus were still a small minority in the Roman Empire by about the year 100. But they were growing in number and increasingly visible. One notable and often-cited example of the growing awareness of the Jesus Movement came in the year 112, when a provincial governor named Pliny (the same Pliny who wrote the most famous account of the destruction of Pompeii) wrote to Emperor Trajan (the same Trajan who presided over the Roman Empire's greatest extent, as I noted above). To make a long story short, some followers of Jesus had been denounced and turned over to Pliny, and he wasn't sure what to do with them. He wrote to Trajan to ask for advice and instructions and to find out whether being a follower of Jesus was, by itself, enough to make someone a criminal. Trajan's response was that governors like Pliny should not seek out Jesus' followers: there should be no general rule that being a Christian would be illegal. But, Trajan continued, if someone denounced a follower of Jesus to the Roman state and Pliny had the opportunity to interrogate them, then devotion to Jesus—if proven—should be punished.

This exchange between Pliny and Trajan gives us a window into the way the Roman government was thinking about Jesus' followers in the years and decades around and after Acts was written and the ways the new Jesus Movement was interacting with the Roman state. In some ways the words of Pliny and Trajan are evenhanded and reassuring; they were not trying to purge Christians from the Roman Empire, as is often imagined. But in other ways their words are chilling and they confirm that some of the Roman Empire's power—some of its violence, its economic strength, its social structures—could be wielded like a weapon against Christians.

As a way to conclude this introduction, let's turn to the Roman Empire itself: what it was, how it worked, and how it was—and *was not*—like the world in which we live today.

Imperium, Authoritarianism, and Autocracy

Historians often warn against anachronism: they remind us that the past is not the same as the present and that we should be careful not to equate them too much. We live in vastly different circumstances, with dramatically different experiences, and inside of starkly different cultures and governmental systems than did the people living in the first and second centuries in the Roman Empire. While many people *do* compare the United States to the Roman Empire—in both flattering and unflattering ways—history does not repeat itself. The history of the Roman Empire is one thing, and our world is a very different thing, even if we can sometimes see parallels.

In this book, I want to pay attention to those parallels without claiming anything too grandiose about the relationship between the past and the present. As Mark Twain is purported to have said, "history doesn't repeat itself, but it often rhymes." It's the rhyming that interests me, and even if the world of Acts and the world in which we live are not very much alike, the Book of Acts can be a useful guide to making sense of our own place and time.

For many of us, the Bible is a sacred text that speaks out of the past and into our lives in the present. Many of us are accustomed to thinking about the Bible as a kind of mirror in which we can see ourselves and our circumstances, even if the Bible describes a world that's very different than ours. As I have watched the changes in the United States over the past decade or so, especially since Donald Trump's rise to political power, I have often found myself thinking about Acts as a guide, as a set of parallels that rhyme with the events of the present. I spend the rest of this book paying attention to the parallels and the rhymes. But I want to start here by pointing out some big-picture similarities—and differences—between the world of Acts and our own world.

The largest and most important similarity is autocratic and authoritarian government, and all that autocracy and authoritarianism bring. Each chapter of this book focuses on a different aspect of autocracy and authoritarianism that tends to hold true across time and place. These include things like governmental corruption, the uses of history to justify actions in the present, the seizure and control of territory, the marginalization of some people and groups, unjust criminal justice systems and weaponized incarceration, the normalization and use of violence as a political means, and the ways autocracies protect and use money, to name a few of the themes in the chapters that follow.

The Book of Acts is full of examples of how the Roman Empire, as an autocratic state, engaged in those activities and used authoritarian tactics to achieve its ends. The headlines and news alerts of our own twenty-first-century world are likewise full of examples that fit those categories. When we hear about ICE agents rounding up and deporting people without any evidence of wrongdoing, or worse, even *despite* evidence that the person is in the United States legally, for example, we can notice that those events *rhyme* with the way Paul was mistaken for a rebellious Egyptian in Acts 21:37 and mistreated because of it. When we hear about people trying to influence the United States government by steering business toward the president and members of the administration, we notice the rhyme with the way local economic protectionism played a critical role in Acts 16 and 19. When we see the American prison system with its rampant racial disparities and record of ineffective rehabilitation, we hear the rhyme with Paul's experiences of imprisonment in the latter chapters of Acts. We will look closely at all those stories and many more in the chapters to come, and we will have a chance to see how Acts tells its story as a way of resisting the actions of an autocratic state and the tactics of authoritarian rule.

Whether you are interested in resistance to your government's actions, understanding how autocratic governments work, or simply learning more about the Bible and the world from which it comes, the chapters that follow offer something for you. We will turn a keen eye on the systems of power and control that Acts describes and also on the ways some of those same systems show up in our world today. We will bear witness to how power affected the lives of people in the stories of Acts and also think about how power works in our own lives. We will ask—as one character in Acts asks of Peter and John early in the book—"by what power" the events of Acts unfold, and we will ask the same of our own time and place. And we will discover, as the people who inhabit the Book of Acts did, that every form of power has its limits.

Further Reading

In this chapter and the ones that follow, I will add footnotes to certain claims so you will know where I am getting my information. But for the most part I will cite sparsely to avoid breaking up the flow of the text. Instead, I'll add a section like this one at the end of each chapter, pointing to some of my favorite resources and scholarship for exploring things further.

This first section is the Introduction, so I will take this opportunity to point you toward some good introductions to the Book of Acts, including good resources for thinking about some of the claims I have made here about things like the authorship and dating of Acts. One of my favorite recent commentaries on Acts is Willie James Jennings' volume *Acts* in the *Belief* series.[3] Jennings is a theologian by training, not a Bible scholar, and that makes his commentary especially rich in theological reflection. Jennings pays close attention to the ways power—both divine and political—flows through the Book of Acts.

Earlier I cited a wonderful little book by Justo González called *The Story Luke Tells*.[4] This, too, is a fairly theological reading of the Book of Acts alongside its companion volume, the Gospel of Luke. Part of González's framing is that he sees Luke as consistently calling for and anticipating a general inversion of the world's power structures—a *last become first* change that he calls "the great reversal." And Shelly Matthews has written a powerful handbook titled *The*

---

[3] Willie James Jennings, *Acts: A Theological Commentary on the Bible* (Westminster John Knox, 2017).

[4] González, *The Story Luke Tells*.

Acts of the Apostles: Taming the Tongues of Fire.[5] Matthews is renowned for her work on martyrdom, so her book will be especially useful if you want to delve deeper into Acts' stories about violence.

If you are looking for a general introduction that covers the basics, like the Book of Acts' dating and authorship, then George Shillington's book *An Introduction to the Study of Luke-Acts* is solid and accessible.[6] You can find a more comprehensive approach in Carl R. Holladay's *Acts: A Commentary*, which is a useful guide to nearly every major scholarly debate.[7] And if you find yourself wanting to learn most of everything scholars have ever said about Acts or anything related, you won't do better than Craig S. Keener's massive and exhaustive four-volume set *Acts: An Exegetical Commentary*, which spans thousands of pages.[8]

---

[5] Shelly Matthews, *The Acts of the Apostles: Taming the Tongues of Fire*, Phoenix Guides to the New Testament 5 (Sheffield Phoenix Press, 2013).

[6] V. George Shillington, *An Introduction to the Study of Luke-Acts*, 2nd ed. (Bloomsbury, 2015).

[7] Carl R. Holladay, *Acts: A Commentary*, The New Testament Library (Westminster John Knox, 2016).

[8] Craig S. Keener, *Acts: An Exegetical Commentary*, 1: Introduction and 1:1–2:47 (Baker Academic, 2012); Craig S. Keener, *Acts: An Exegetical Commentary*, 2: 3:1–14:28 (Baker Academic, 2013); Craig S. Keener, *Acts: An Exegetical Commentary*, 3: 15:1–23:35 (Baker Academic, 2014); Craig S. Keener, *Acts: An Exegetical Commentary*, 4: 24:1–28:31 (Baker Academic, 2015).

PART I

The Conditions of Autocracy and Empire

Part I of this book focuses on the ways autocratic systems work—both the features that define them and the strategies they employ to maintain power. It contains four chapters: chapter 1 focusing on corruption, chapter 2 looking at the uses of history to justify the present and the future, chapter 3 on the way in which empires covet territory, and chapter 4 considering the ways autocratic systems and empires place some people at the center of importance and others at the edges. Each of these chapters takes a broad view of how power flows through systems, both today and in the past. Each one notices how the Book of Acts describes patterns familiar to us in the present.

1

Corruption

The first time I remember hearing about a corrupt government official, I was about ten years old. Most nights my parents watched the news on TV at 6:30—always Tom Brokaw because our antenna could only pick up two broadcast channels, and NBC was one of them. In the mid- to late 1980s, on many nights the news included a segment about a man named Ferdinand Marcos. As a kid, I didn't know much about Marcos or the country where he was president, the Philippines. But I could tell that Marcos was a controversial figure because Tom Brokaw always wore his most serious scowl and used a scolding voice when talking about him.

Ferdinand Marcos was president of the Philippines for about twenty years, from the mid-1960s until 1986. As president, Marcos was notorious for several abuses of power, including human rights violations, media censorship, and violence against his opponents. He also presided over a roller coaster of an economy and some revisions to the country's constitution that helped concentrate power in his own hands. There was enough drama during Marcos' presidency to keep Tom Brokaw busy most nights when the news came on. But the strongest memory I have from that time, as an impressionable kid, is of hearing about the way Marcos stole money from his own country to fund a lavish lifestyle.

As a young person living a long way away from anyone who was either wealthy or powerful, I didn't have much of a frame of reference for what Marcos was doing. But I do remember one small detail that they kept repeating on the news each night: that at the end of Ferdinand Marcos' presidency, after he and his wife, Imelda, fled the country in a hurry, it was discovered that Imelda owned over a thousand pairs of shoes. This made a big impression on me as a kid because I never had more than a couple of pairs of shoes at a time, tops. I couldn't imagine having a thousand pairs of shoes, and those shoes became a symbol in my mind of what a corrupt government looked like. Since then, journalists and scholars have estimated that Ferdinand and Imelda Marcos stole billions of dollars from the Philippines to fund their lifestyle and enrich their families and friends.

Marcos called his style of government "constitutional authoritarianism," which was his way of arguing that everything he did was permitted by the rules. And in some sense, he might have been right. In authoritarian or autocratic systems, the leader is often conflated with the nation in that way: the interests of the leader *are* the interests of the state, so anything the leader wants to do should be permitted. And sometimes the financial interests of the nation become entangled with the financial interests of the nation's leader so that the government itself becomes a way for the leader to make money. Political theorists have another word for this kind of system: *kleptocracy*. A kleptocracy (derived from the Greek word for stealing) is a system of government in which the leaders steal from the country and the people. Kleptocratic leaders use their power to enrich themselves and their allies by skimming off the top of normal government activities and transactions, fixing contracts so they go to their cronies, taking bribes and kickbacks, and engaging in outright embezzlement.

The thousand pairs of shoes represented only a small portion of the money that Marcos stole from the Philippines, but the shoes were a potent symbol of corruption. The Marcos family was living an extravagant lifestyle while many ordinary Filipinos struggled economically, and eventually—in a movement called the People Power Revolution—Marcos was forced from power and sent into exile in Hawaii. But Marcos was not the first leader to enrich himself through corruption, and he would not be the last.

What Is Corruption?

Simply speaking, government corruption happens when the line blurs between public and private roles. Every national and political leader is also a private person, with their own private finances, family connections, friendships, and commitments. One principle of normal, good national leadership is that the leader of a country ought to act in the best interests of the country and not of themselves. Everyone who serves in public office comes to the role with their own history and principles and a list of things they want to accomplish; that is normal. What is *not* normal is for a role in government to be more about serving oneself or one's family than about serving the nation. Many modern democracies insist that leaders put their financial assets into a blind trust so that other people are managing the leader's finances and the leader cannot manipulate financial markets or contracts for personal gain. Other countries require that leaders divest themselves completely from certain kinds of assets that might be especially vulnerable to corruption. These rules are in place to ensure that when a leader—like a president—makes a decision, they make the decision in the best interest of the people and not themselves, their family, or their cronies.

Corruption happens when that line between public and private gets blurred or when the line is erased altogether. The word *corruption* assumes that the system is supposed to be fair and that leaders are supposed to work on behalf of the public and not themselves. The word *corruption* then describes times when the proper functioning of the system has become *corrupted* or damaged and is no longer working as it is supposed to. Corruption can be financial (leaders stealing money, like Marcos did), or it can involve leaders wielding and trading influence or power improperly. The word *kleptocracy* refers to what happens when the system itself is set up for graft and theft—when the whole system is so dominated by corruption that theft becomes not the exception but the rule. We could think of the case of Ferdinand Marcos in the Philippines as a case of corruption (Marcos was breaking the rules in order to enrich himself) that morphed into a case of kleptocracy (Marcos changed the rules so that the system benefitted him and his allies). The distinction between a corrupt system and a kleptocracy might not matter much to the people who are being fleeced by their own leaders, but at least in cases of corruption there are potentially consequences for the leaders' actions. Corrupt leaders still feasibly face scrutiny for how they break the rules. A kleptocracy normalizes theft, and everyone assumes that a position of political leadership is an opportunity for self-enrichment. The difference between them is found in the norms and whether people expect the system to be corrupt.

In the United States, corruption scandals are common at every level of government and across political parties, though they have been increasingly frequent in recent years. Not long after the time when I was watching Tom Brokaw talking about Ferdinand Marcos on the news, I remember learning about the Teapot Dome scandal in my history class at school. In that scandal, which happened during the administration of President Warren G. Harding in the 1920s, Secretary of the Interior Albert B. Fall took bribes to direct oil leases to coconspirators at unfairly low rates. Fall ended up being convicted of taking bribes and was sent to prison. More recently, President Bill Clinton was criticized for allowing political donors and friends to stay in the Lincoln Bedroom as a reward for their support, thereby using a public asset to benefit private citizens. The administration of Donald Trump has supercharged accusations of corruption in government, with Trump engaging in a number of actions that his critics say blur the lines between Trump as a private citizen and Trump as a representative of the American people. Breaking long tradition, Trump declined to divest himself of his assets, including many businesses (like hotels) that made it easy for people to funnel money in his direction and win favor with him. He accepted the donation of a jet plane from the Qatari government valued at hundreds of millions of dollars (to be outfitted by the United States government at a cost of millions more), and Trump has said that the jet will be donated to his own presidential library following his presidency—essentially turning the jet into Trump's private asset. To Trump's critics, the list of the ways he has practiced corruption is too long to detail here.

Of course, corruption happens at levels far below the presidency. One feature of kleptocracies is that once people understand that the people at the top are on the take, the whole system becomes corrupt. Everyone—from customs officials to drivers' license officers to police to building inspectors to business regulators to Supreme Court justices—begins to look for ways to enrich themselves through their role. Citizens might find themselves paying bribes as part of everyday life, and companies begin to build the costs of cronyism into the costs of doing business. When corruption is normalized, it becomes a part of how things are done, a corruption tax on everything, and everyone begins to accept that that's just the way the system works. Eventually, for example, someone who has been arrested might find that the outcome of their case depends not on their guilt or innocence but on their ability to pay a bribe to the police, jailers, or judges who control their fate. That is, in fact, precisely what happened to the apostle Paul in the latter chapters of Acts.

How Does Corruption Show Up in Acts?

Say what you will about the apostle Paul—and there is a lot to say about him, both positive and negative—but Paul does *not* appear to have been stupid. Paul had a restless intelligence that comes across in his letters, but it might be even more prominent in the Acts of the Apostles, which describes him as wily, resourceful, slippery, savvy, street-smart, and driven. In Acts, Paul always seems to be one step ahead of whoever is trying to get in his way, and Paul always seems to find his way out of tight spots. So it's telling that at the end of chapter 24, Paul realized he was trapped.

Paul came to this realization as he was being held in custody of the Roman Empire, first by a governor named Felix and then by his successor, Festus. The circumstances of Paul's confinement are a little bit confusing and convoluted, as we will see both in this chapter and later in this book. (Similarly, I will have a lot more to say about both ancient criminal justice systems and imprisonment in later chapters. We will return to this part of Acts as a window through which we can peer to see how incarceration and trials worked in the ancient world and how they work today.) In this chapter, though, I want to focus on the story of Paul's arrest and imprisonment and trials, as told in chapters 21 to 25 of Acts, and four different moments of government corruption that appear in those verses. Those chapters give us insight into the ways Acts tells us about government corruption and the ways corruption was—and is—a fact of life under systems of government like the one Paul faced. Like many people caught in the courts and prisons of authoritarian and imperial governments everywhere, Paul's experiences of corruption eventually led him to lose hope that he could receive any impartial justice. Paul was smart enough to figure out that nobody inside the Roman criminal justice system had his best interests in mind. He was smart enough to realize he was trapped.

Acts 21 to 24 are remarkable chapters because they tell the story of Paul's arrest and imprisonment with a breathtaking honesty that makes the Roman Empire look bumbling at best and blatantly immoral at worst. It's surprising that the author of Acts felt free to criticize the empire so openly, but these chapters do not pull any punches. In moment after moment, the author of Acts shows the representatives of that empire to be self-serving and dishonest and sometimes incompetent. The devastating way Acts tells the story of arrest and imprisonment will be familiar to many people who have interacted with corrupt governments. Once Paul was ensnared in the system, it became almost impossible for him to get out again or even to understand what actions he could take to try to make that happen. Paul found himself trapped in the maddening contradictions of a kleptocratic state, in which his guilt and innocence did not matter as much as the private interests of the government officials who controlled his fate and Paul's ability to serve those interests.

The story of government corruption is a critical part of why Paul was trapped, as Acts tells it. In these chapters—Acts 21 to 24—the author of Acts describes three distinct moments of corruption by government officials, each of which contributes to Paul's entanglement in the Roman justice system and each of which makes it harder for him to escape. These three moments—involving a tribune's dishonesty, a governor's search for a bribe, and that same governor's use of a prisoner as a bargaining chip—portray the Roman government in Judea in a rather poor light. But for people living in corrupt or kleptocratic systems, especially in areas that have been conquered by an empire and are being governed from a distance, the story of what happened to Paul might sound familiar. Let's take these instances of corruption one at a time and ask what they can tell us about life in these kinds of systems.

The first instance of corruption, the one involving a tribune's dishonesty, comes early in the story of Paul's troubles in Jerusalem, so we will start at the beginning of this section and follow the action as it unfolds. Chapter 21 picks up with Paul in Jerusalem. How did he get there, and why was he there? As Acts tells it, Paul had just returned to the eastern part of the Mediterranean, where

Jerusalem is, after a long journey westward into Asia Minor and Greece—one of what many modern Christians call Paul's "missionary journeys." In Jerusalem, "James, and all the elders" (21:18) greeted Paul, and those elders told Paul about what had been happening in Judea and Jerusalem during his absence. People were likely to be suspicious about Paul, the elders told him, because of rumors that he had been teaching Jews in the diaspora not to follow the Jewish law. And everyone likely would learn quickly that he was in town, the elders told Paul, so it would be best for him to get ahead of the story. What better way to show allegiance to the Jewish law and the deep history of Jewish tradition than to visit the temple and perform a ritual? Paul likely eagerly agreed to the plan. Throughout his letters, whenever he has a chance, Paul affirms the value of Judaism and his ongoing commitment to it, so this story from Acts is very much in character for Paul. Paul agreed to sponsor a quartet of men who were undergoing a rite of purification as part of a religious vow. So the next day they all went to the temple together. And soon everything fell apart.

Paul did *not* receive a warm welcome in the temple. James and the elders were right: it seems that many people *did* view Paul with deep suspicion. Acts tells the story of a group of Jews—Jews who, like Paul, are from the diaspora, or Jews living out in the cities of the Roman Empire instead of in Judea—seizing Paul and shouting accusations about him. (More on diaspora in the next chapter.) This led to quite a scene in which Paul was dragged from the temple precincts and, as Acts tells it, the crowd was trying to kill him. At this point, this was an intra-religious conflict, a dispute between and among Jews about the right and proper way to understand and practice Judaism, and it was spiraling out of control. It was certainly a dangerous moment for Paul, but for now he was arguing with other Jews about how to be Jewish, and Rome was not yet involved.

That all changes at the end of chapter 21 when "the tribune of the cohort" (v. 31) named Claudius Lysias heard that "all Jerusalem was in an uproar." Claudius, who was the presiding military officer—the representative of Rome charged with keeping the peace in and around the temple—heard reports about the dispute (which to him probably looked like a riot) and intervened by arresting Paul and having him bound. Paul and the tribune then had a conversation about Paul's identity—a telling exchange to which we will return in a later chapter. As part of that exchange, Paul launched into a long speech defending himself and his actions. At the end of the speech, the crowd became enraged, and the tribune—no doubt trying to placate the crowd—ordered Paul to be flogged as a way of interrogating him. At that moment, Paul asked an extremely powerful rhetorical question: "Is it legal for you to flog a Roman person who is uncondemned?" (22:25).

It is a powerful question because the answer is no: it was *not* legal for anyone to flog a Roman citizen who had not been legally condemned. Furthermore, it was not even legal for the tribune Claudius to have bound Paul earlier when he had had him arrested. The Roman Empire was starkly organized into social strata, and different rules applied to different classes of people. For a non-citizen like Jesus, and especially for someone at the very bottom of the social structure like an enslaved person, there were few restrictions on the kinds of punishments and bodily restraints that could be imposed. But for someone holding Roman citizenship, which is what Paul claimed to have when he asked his rhetorical question, the rules were a lot stricter. Citizens stood closer to the top of the social order, and officials couldn't just arrest and bind them willy-nilly. You can see the severity of the situation in Acts 22:29, where "immediately those who were about to examine him drew back from him; and the tribune also was afraid." All at once, everyone in the situation became aware that they had been playing by a set of rules that did not apply and that they were all in danger of being punished for the careless way they had been treating Paul.

Paul's question about whether it was proper to bind citizens did get him out of immediate danger. Claudius and his soldiers took Paul into custody, put him in front of a Jerusalem council (more on this in a moment), and then—most of a chapter later—Claudius sent Paul to his boss, Felix. Felix was the governor of the province of Judea (the Latin term would have been *procurator*), and he was responsible for administering the province and representing the Roman Empire's interests there. Claudius Lysias reported to Felix, so when he sent Paul to see him, Claudius sent a short letter along with him, which the author of Acts includes in 23:26–30. There is no way to know whether this is actually the word-for-word letter that Claudius sent or how Luke might have gotten hold of it, but many scholars seem to believe it is genuine. As Acts records it, the letter read:

> Claudius Lysias to his Excellency the governor Felix, greetings. This man was seized by the Jews and was about to be killed by them, but when I had learned that he was a Roman, I came with the guard and rescued him. Since I wanted to know the charge for which they accused him, I had him brought to their council. I found that he was accused concerning questions of their law but was charged with nothing deserving death or imprisonment. When I was informed that there would be a plot against the man, I sent him to you at once, ordering his accusers also to state before you what they have against him.

You might notice right away that Claudius Lysias told the story of Paul's arrest a little differently than Luke told it. The way Claudius told the story, *he* was the hero who swooped in to rescue Paul from certain death. But in the way Acts tells the story, the tribune arrested Paul on the assumption that he was an Egyptian rebel (more about that in a coming chapter). For his letter to his boss Felix, Claudius turned himself into the hero who did the right thing from the beginning, rather than the careless law enforcement officer who treated Paul without respect and failed to do his due diligence regarding Paul's identity. In fact, Claudius completely left out the part where he tied Paul up and prepared to flog him, and he pretended that he had always been aware that Paul was a citizen—a "Roman," as he put it in his letter. Instead of telling the story of how he was about to resort to violence against Paul, Claudius Lysias instead cast himself as Paul's protector, telling Felix he had sent Paul onward for his own safety.

How is this corruption? Claudius was not seeking financial benefit, at least not directly. Instead, Claudius was engaging in a kind of government cover-up—a retelling of the story that hid the truth and made him look good and noble in the eyes of his superiors. Claudius was twisting the story of Paul's arrest to benefit his own career and not carrying out a duty to truth or to Paul as an accused person. As a government official, Claudius was in a position to twist the official record to suit his own purposes, and he did so, dodging blame for his mistakes and taking credit for things he never did.

The second instance of corruption in this section is the most blatant. In Paul's imprisonment under the governor Felix, we can clearly see the ways corruption interfered in the proper workings of government and deprived people of their rights. Once Felix had received Paul and the letter from Claudius, he arranged for a hearing, and the high priest Ananias came with some other elders and an attorney named Tertullus. Felix heard the arguments from Tertullus and the accusations against Paul, which basically boiled down to the idea that Paul was an agitator and a threat to public safety. Then Felix asked Paul to defend himself, and Paul argued against the charges of being a rabble-rouser and reiterated his allegiance to the Jewish law. At the end of that trial, in a scene that included Felix's wife, Drusilla, Acts gives the readers some insight into Felix's thinking. "Go away for the present," Felix tells Paul. "When I have an opportunity, I will send for you" (24:25). But the narrator of Acts tells us, in an aside, that Felix "hoped that money would be given him by Paul, and for that reason he used to send for him very often and converse with him." Felix wanted a bribe.

From our modern perspective, this was an egregious breach of justice, even if we can recognize elements of it in the way our own systems of justice work (or don't work). Instead of carrying out the work of justice and adjudicating

Paul's case in an efficient and just way, Felix put off making a ruling because he was hoping Paul would pay him a bribe. This detail will be familiar to anyone who has lived under a corrupt system: even if you are innocent, you can be kept in prison if you aren't able to pay a bribe to the judge or jailer. (Later, in chapter 5, we will talk about criminal justice systems and the ways those systems do not always seek justice in the ways we might hope.) But even if we grant that any system of justice will be imperfect and that people in the system might have many motivations beyond the pure concerns of justice, what happens in those two verses is shocking. Felix keeps Paul in custody because he thinks he can personally profit from doing so, and he avoids carrying out his duty because if he did, he would lose his ability to make some money.

But it gets worse. In the third instance of corruption, in the last verse of the chapter, the narrator drops a very important detail: "After two years had passed," Acts says in 24:27, "Felix was succeeded by Porcius Festus, and since he wanted to grant the Jews a favor, Felix left Paul in prison." In other words, two years after Paul was arrested, Felix's term as governor was over, and a new governor named Festus was taking office. That would have been a good opportunity for Felix to release Paul or else find him guilty, since he would no longer be in a position to profit personally from Paul's imprisonment. But instead, Felix left Paul in prison as a favor for the people who had accused Paul in the first place. Acts doesn't tell us much about Paul's condition or mindset at this point, but it's easy to imagine that after two years of imprisonment he had become frustrated, angry, or resigned to his fate. Once he was caught in the machinery of the Roman justice system, Paul stopped being in control of his own life and his freedom was held hostage because of the profits and favors being cultivated by a person in a position of power.

So from the time he was arrested in Jerusalem in the temple, Paul's life became a bargaining chip in the hands of corrupt government officials. The tribune Claudius Lysias twisted Paul's story to make himself look better. The governor Felix tried to extort a bribe from Paul in exchange for his freedom. Then after two years Felix left Paul in prison, rather than properly adjudicating his case, because Paul's ongoing imprisonment was more valuable to Felix than justice would have been. For Felix, it was easier to use Paul as a way of paying off a favor than it was simply to do his job. Once Paul entered the justice system, he was at the whims of people who were looking out for themselves—people who were more interested in how they could profit personally from their position and their power than they were in properly carrying out their role. That's the definition of government corruption.

Living with Corruption

We don't know how Paul's story turned out, really. The Book of Acts followed Paul as far as it could. In the next chapter, after Felix decided to leave Paul in prison, Paul made an appeal to the Roman emperor—something Roman citizens apparently had the right to do. In doing so, Paul was probably placing a bet on the emperor being less partial and more interested in justice than the tribune and the governor were, or maybe too wealthy to be influenced by a bribe. Whether that was a good bet or not, we will never know, because the Book of Acts concludes Paul's story a few chapters later in Rome, with Paul under house arrest in Rome and still waiting for his audience with the emperor. We don't know what happened to Paul—whether he was exonerated, punished somehow, or executed. Local Roman tradition has it that Paul was executed, and that tradition might be correct because his trail runs cold at that point; we don't have any letters or any other writings from Paul after his journey to Rome. If Luke knew what happened to Paul, he didn't put it in his book.

Paul's story probably didn't have a happy ending, and most of the other stories of people caught up by government corruption don't have happy endings either. If your freedom, your livelihood, your safety, or your life depends on a corrupt government official doing the right thing, then you are in danger. Corruption is so troubling because it takes the normal functioning of government and twists it so that it doesn't serve the needs of everyday people, but it instead serves the needs of the few people who are able to secure positions of power. It might seem relatively harmless for a police officer to take a bribe to change a speeding ticket to a warning or for a president to accept an extravagant gift from a foreign government, but the consequences go far beyond money. As Paul's story demonstrates, good government depends on the people in positions of power acting in the best interests of the public and making decisions based on the rule of law and the common good. When that ceases to be true—when the people in power begin to think first of themselves and their own fortunes—things tend to go really wrong.

How, then, should we act if we find ourselves confronted with government corruption? I think Paul's story from Acts holds at least a couple of lessons for us. The first lesson has to do with the value of honesty and transparency, as once those virtues disappear from public servants, they can be hard to retrieve. Imagine how Paul's story might have turned out differently if there had been a journalist creating a real-time account of Paul's arrest and treatment under Claudius Lysias and the ways in which his story to Felix didn't match up with what had actually happened. Imagine how the story might have been different if there had been a watchdog keeping tabs on how Felix's actions did or did not honor the rights of prisoners and holding him to account for the speedy administration of justice. These are modern ideas (a free press and the right to a speedy and fair trial), but they are some of the institutions that protect us from the abuses of corrupt officials. The only reason we know about the actions of these corrupt Roman officials toward Paul at all is that Luke wrote about them. We can never rely on insiders to make us aware of their own corruption. Watchdogs, a free press, and transparent systems of justice are critical to fighting corruption.

The second lesson has to do with scale and connection and not letting things slide. It can be hard to see the connection between big corrupt systems and the ways those systems affect your everyday life. And likewise, it can feel daunting to try to keep track of how small acts of corruption—a favor here, a no-bid contract there—can add up to a crisis. But when we think about corruption as a pattern, we can begin to see the connections between the small things (Claudius Lysias' revisionist history when he told the story of Paul's arrest) and the big things (Felix trading away Paul's freedom for a political favor and the hope of a bribe). They don't have a lot to do with each other, but they are connected to each other and to other big-picture patterns of corruption that Acts doesn't talk about—things like Roman governors being chosen for their political connections rather than for their skill in administration. In systems, the large scale is connected to the small scale, and the small and large influence each other. Corruption, too, can travel quickly from big-time to small-time and back again.

In the Philippines, the corruption of the Marcos regime was eventually stamped out by a popular rebellion. Through a series of dramatic developments, the People Power Revolution and its allies ousted Marcos and sent him into exile. But the story was not over. Echoes of Marcos' corruption continue to reverberate in the Philippines, and smaller-scale scandals have popped up in Filipino government ever since, demonstrating that once it takes hold, corruption can be very difficult to eradicate. In the Philippines and elsewhere, protecting against corruption requires vigilance, transparency, and accountability on the part of citizens, the press, and government institutions. Without those things, government can become just another way for someone to make a dollar.

As the Teapot Dome scandal shows, the American system of government has always been vulnerable to corruption, but it has also found ways to push back against it and keep officials accountable to the people. It remains to be seen whether that will continue to be true in the future, as President Trump uses the trappings of his office to funnel money to his and his family members' businesses, to solicit extravagant gifts from foreign governments in violation of the Emoluments Clause of the Constitution, and to seek and sometimes win large settlements from news organizations like CBS and the BBC when they run unfavorable stories about him.[1] The example of the Philippines shows that even if the United States historically has had low levels of government corruption, once corruption takes hold, it can be difficult to get rid of it. And in the Trump presidency, corruption is taking hold at the highest levels and at rates unprecedented in American history.

Further Reading

In recent years, scholars of the Book of Acts have been very excited about a new book by Jeremy L. Williams, titled *Criminalization in the Acts of the Apostles: Race, Rhetoric, and the Prosecution of an Early Christian Movement.*[2] Williams spends a lot of time focusing on the same part of Acts that this chapter does: Paul's encounter with Claudius Lysias. Williams' scholarship relies heavily on his new translations of some of the terms found in this section, in which he replaces unfamiliar terms like *tribune* and *cohort* with more familiar ones like *police captain* and *militarized police*. By doing so, he helps us to see the parallels between the kinds of violence Paul experienced as a prisoner of Rome and the systems by which people are oppressed in our own place and time.

Matthew L. Skinner has a couple of great books that help us get a sense of the realities behind Paul's experiences as they are told in Acts. *The Trial Narratives: Conflict, Power, and Identity in the New Testament* helps us to see how Acts is negotiating Roman imperial power in these scenes.[3] And in *Locating Paul: Places of Custody as Narrative Settings in Acts 21–28*, Skinner pays attention to how Acts portrays Roman systems of justice.[4] Reaching back a few decades earlier, Brian Rapske's *The Book of Acts and Paul in Roman Custody* shows us the inner workings of Roman judicial systems.[5]

---

[1] Lazaro Gamio and Amy Schoenfeld Walker, "Trump's Tangled Web of Deal-Making, Policy and Riches," *New York Times*, December 31, 2025, https://www.nytimes.com/interactive/2025/12/31/us/trump-deals-policy-conflicts-web.html?smid=nytcore-ios-share.

[2] Jeremy L. Williams, *Criminalization in the Acts of the Apostles: Race, Rhetoric, and the Prosecution of an Early Christian Movement* (Cambridge University Press, 2023).

[3] Matthew L. Skinner, *The Trial Narratives: Conflict, Power, and Identity in the New Testament* (Westminster John Knox, 2010).

[4] Matthew L. Skinner, *Locating Paul: Places of Custody as Narrative Settings in Acts 21–28* (Society of Biblical Literature, 2003).

[5] Brian Rapske, *The Book of Acts and Paul in Roman Custody*, vol. 3, The Book of Acts in Its First-Century Setting (William B. Eerdmans and The Paternoster Press, 1994).

2

History

I grew up in the old territory of the Confederacy. Between the ages of three and twenty-eight, I lived in North Carolina and Tennessee: first in a small town near North Carolina's border with Virginia, then near Asheville while I was in college, in Nashville where I went to graduate school, and in Johnson City where my wife earned her MFA. Although I was born and spent the first few years of my life on an Air Force base in New Jersey, I have very little memory of that time. All my formative years were spent in the South, and all my early cultural and educational experiences were filtered through the way the people in the South understood their history and told the stories of the past.

Reflecting on my childhood now, I can see that much of my formation as a person in the South happened in the background and was invisible to me. As a White person growing up there, no one ever sat me down and explained race to me or told me how I should think about the region's past. Nobody ever instructed me to sympathize with the Confederacy or to view different races with discrimination—least of all my parents, who were always careful to teach me by words and example the importance of seeing everyone as equals and who denounced blatant racism when they saw it.

Instead, I was formed as a White person in the South bit by bit, usually by suggestion and innuendo. Today, with hindsight, I can see the ways the histories of the region and the people were told with a slanted point of view. My school history classes were sometimes taught by people who, upon later reflection, emphasized what is often called the "Lost Cause" view of the Civil War. It was not at all uncommon to see Confederate flags on the side of the road or on the T-shirts of other kids at school. We took field trips to old plantations and toured the grand old houses and the slave quarters, but no one once mentioned to me that our very town had once been a plantation itself. (I wonder how many of them knew.) The county's best picnic spot was at a riverside park featuring the remains of an old iron furnace that had once churned out weaponry for the Confederate army. All those things added up in a way that I can only recognize from my current perspective as a grown person who lives a long way away. Together, the conditions of my childhood conspired to teach me something about history and my place in the world. Most people never said White nationalist or White supremacist things out loud, but my world was put together in a way that made believing those things possible.

For instance, when I was a kid, my father was stationed at an Air Force base adjacent to the giant army base called Fort Bragg in east-central North Carolina, and I spent a decent amount of time there. I never wondered who the Bragg was in the Fort Bragg name; it turns out he was a Confederate general who had been honored in the naming of an Army base. Or, to take another example, when I was about thirteen years old in 1990, our county's local Sons of Confederate Veterans and the county historical society installed a monument "IN HONOR OF ALL WHO SERVED," carved from red granite and featuring a version of the Confederate flag but not the American flag. The county to the east of ours had a similar monument, dating from 1910. (A car hit and destroyed it in 2011, and the monument was replaced in 2014.) The county to the west of ours didn't have a monument but installed one in 2005, 140 years after the conclusion of the Civil War. And, in a final example, when I went to college in 1996, I found that the supposedly liberal city of Asheville had its own enormous monument dedicated to a Civil War-era politician and slave owner.

Recent years have seen a lot of controversy about these kinds of naming conventions and monuments. The Black Lives Matter movement and other waves of racial justice activism have drawn attention to the ways monuments and honorary names can normalize and give permission for regressive and hateful views of history. Many of these monuments have been taken down in the last ten years or so, including the one in Asheville in 2021. In 2022 Fort Bragg was renamed Fort Liberty to remove the association with a person who had openly fought against the United States and for the Confederacy. But in early 2025, Secretary of Defense Pete Hegseth reversed the decision and restored the name of Fort Bragg, saying that the base would now be named after a different Bragg, one who was a hero of the Second World War, rather than the Confederate general—though the distinction likely will be lost on many people who complained when the Bragg name was removed in the first place. In the fall of 2025, pursuant to an executive order that the president signed earlier in the year, the Trump Administration reinstalled a Washington, D.C., statue of a Confederate general that protesters had toppled in 2020. In that 2025 executive order, Trump wrote that restoring monuments would help in "restoring truth and sanity to American history," arguing that removal of the statues was "undermining the remarkable achievements of the United States by casting its founding principles and historical milestones in a negative light."[1]

What does all this have to do with Acts? Though we might think of history as facts and dates that live in books somewhere, history is actually much more alive than that. History is a practice of storytelling; history is the way we tell the story of ourselves by telling stories about the past. Autocrats and authoritarians have long recognized that history is a powerful way to motivate people and consolidate power. A monument or a sign or a T-shirt with a reference to a Confederate general or flag might not seem very powerful at first, but together they tell a story about the world and the places of various kinds of people in that world.

As a kid, I absorbed a lot of the story that I was being shown and told—not an overtly racist story, but a story that tried to frame the Confederacy as a misunderstood and tragic time of lost beauty and honor. It wasn't until later, once I learned other ways of telling the story from other kinds of storytellers, that I was able to see how much power that way of talking about the past had over me and the people around me.

We often think of history as something that has to do with the past, but that's not always true. History can be a very useful way to speak into the present and the future. Many autocrats use history to justify their actions, and these days it's increasingly common to see various forms of nationalism that are rooted in appeals to history. Nationalism, as we will see, depends on a certain telling of history—a telling that constructs and represents the nation's past as a lost glorious age that must be restored. Many leaders have discovered that by describing (or inventing) a glorious nationalist past, they can hoard power in the present and in the future. Storytelling about the past can be used to justify the seizure of land because the land, those storytellers say, rightly belongs to people who do not currently possess it, but who did possess it in the past or who should possess it again. People can use storytelling about the past to justify violence against minority groups because, many autocrats say, minority groups are invaders who do not truly belong in the nation or its territories and must be expelled in order to reestablish the glorious past. Autocrats use storytelling about the past to rally people to restore something that they claim has been lost or taken away. Let's turn our attention to a few examples from the present and the recent past to see how history gets used to justify actions in the present.

---

[1] Donald J. Trump, "Restoring Truth and Sanity to American History," March 27, 2025, https://www.whitehouse.gov/presidential-actions/2025/03/restoring-truth-and-sanity-to-american-history/.

How Do Autocrats Use History?

When Russia invaded Ukraine in 2022, the shooting war on the ground was preceded and accompanied by a conflict of ideas that played out in television shows, in newspapers, and on social media. While Ukraine had existed in various independent and subjugated states for centuries, and Ukrainians thought of themselves as a unique people with their own language and culture and history, Russian President Vladimir Putin and many other Russians felt differently. Before and leading up to the war, Russian media pushed a narrative that minimized Ukrainian identity, emphasizing the beliefs that Ukrainians are actually Russians and that Ukraine's lands rightfully belong to Russia. They did this using storytelling—they made these claims by turning to history. In fact, several months before Russia invaded Ukraine, Putin himself published a long essay titled *On the Historical Unity of Russians and Ukrainians*. In that essay, Putin argued that Ukraine and Ukrainians are not separate nations and never have been, except as part of an elaborate attack by outsiders meant to harm Russia by peeling off some of its territory. Putin argued that in order to restore Russia's glory in the future, the past would need to be restored and Ukraine and Russia should be united under a broad umbrella of Russian identity. The article was widely viewed as a pretext for the invasion of Ukraine—because if Ukraine were indeed historically a part of Russia, then it would be justifiable to take steps to reunite them. Some critics of Putin's article and his policies even saw it as an apology for genocide, laying the groundwork for the annihilation of Ukrainians. After all, if a people doesn't really exist, then that people can't be destroyed.

Similar uses of history have been deployed in other places. In India, Hindu nationalism understands the Hindu religion as inextricably linked with the people and the land of the Indian subcontinent, and that view of history has been used to marginalize non-Hindus (especially Muslims) and to justify violence against them, claiming that non-Hindus don't really belong anyway. In Israel, the history of the ancient kingdoms of Judah and Israel (and the stories about them found in the Bible) have been used to justify the displacement of Palestinians from their lands, the widespread imprisonment of Palestinian activists, and several wars and outbreaks of violence, most recently following the October 7, 2023, attacks. Both Israelis and Palestinians appeal to history and archaeology to justify their claims and their actions, and neither group seems likely to give up its claims anytime soon. In South Africa the minority White population sometimes has appealed to history to justify apartheid policies, and even today the Trump Administration is repeating those same histories to claim that White South Africans are victims of persecution—claims that South

Africa's government rejects. Meanwhile, in a time when the United States is severely restricting immigration from most countries around the world, the United States has carved out exceptions for White South Africans, saying that their supposed persecuted status makes them worthy asylum seekers.

The United States itself has seen a resurgence of nationalist rhetoric in the past several decades. The people pushing nationalism in the United States—and especially those pushing White nationalism and Christian nationalism—do so by appealing to history. Donald Trump has a great talent for branding things, and perhaps the most successful political branding project of the twenty-first century so far has been his slogan, "Make America Great Again." That slogan, which has been printed on millions of red hats and T-shirts and campaign signs and bumper stickers, tells a story. MAGA is a historical project. It assumes and evokes a particular story—a special way of understanding history—by using the phrase "great again." The implication is that America was great once upon a time (where "greatness" is not defined fully, but left to the imagination of each person), but that its greatness has receded or has been destroyed or undermined. Trump's promise, then, is to restore the lost greatness to America, leaving the details of what that looks like to the imagination of each individual. The means by which Trump has gone about that project—mass deportations, a wholesale gutting of the federal government, and a concentration of power in the executive branch—suggest that, like many other autocrats who make promises to restore a glorious lost past, Trump is using history to reinforce his own grip on power. "Make America Great Again" is another way of saying "Make Trump Powerful," and to a remarkable degree he has gotten his wish.

But there is nothing new under the sun, and recent events in the United States—and in South Africa, Israel, India, Ukraine, and elsewhere—have parallels in the past. As we discussed in the introduction of this book, the Book of Acts can be thought of as a kind of history, and it is making some historical claims that are not so different from some of the ones described above. Today we hear cries of "Make America Great Again," but in the ancient world there were people who wanted to Make Judea Great Again, Make Philippi Great Again, Make Ephesus Great Again, and certainly Make Rome Great Again. We'll turn now to some of those movements and see how they show up in the Book of Acts as it tells its story of the early days of the Jesus Movement.

How Does History Show Up in Acts?

The Book of Acts is indeed itself a form of history, though it is a strange kind of history book by our modern standards. Instead of attempting to describe facts or recreate some version of what actually happened (which is a tall order for *any* work of history, ancient or modern, since history is always contested and fought over), the Book of Acts tries to convince its audience of some things. Acts wants its readers to see the Jesus Movement as heroic and world-changing, and it wants to show how in the aftermath of Jesus' death, his disciples coalesced and organized into a powerful and durable movement. And Acts wants its readers to understand that Jesus is Lord.

Interestingly, the Book of Acts begins with a nationalist and historical question. You might not have noticed it before, but it's right there at the top in the first chapter. In verse 6, the resurrected Jesus appeared among the disciples, and the disciples asked Jesus a question: "Lord, is this the time when you will restore the kingdom to Israel?" That simple question betrays a lot about the disciples' mindset in that moment, and it tells us a lot about their view of history. The disciples had just lived through a very intense time of violence and fear; they had just watched Jesus be arrested, tried, and crucified by the Roman Empire, and now here he is alive again and talking to them. Understandably, the disciples thought they might be living at a pivotal moment in history—a time when Jesus' miraculous resurrection would signal and inaugurate a new period in which Israel's past glory would be renewed. The disciples were in a Make Israel Great Again kind of mood. *Surely*, they were thinking, *now is the moment when the kingdom will be restored?*

The disciples were probably disappointed by Jesus' answer. In verses 7 and 8, Jesus told them that they couldn't know what God had planned for the earthly kingdom of Israel, but that they would become witnesses across the world, speaking about the things they had seen and responding to the promptings of the Holy Spirit. Those verses serve as kind of a thesis statement for the whole Book of Acts; the book does, in fact, tell how the disciples went on to travel across the known world to tell the story of Jesus, all the way over to the city of Rome itself by the time we get to chapter 28. But the disciples' desire in verse 6 went unrealized, and they did not in fact Make Israel Great Again. The hopes they had—that Jesus might become the leader of a newly established nation of Israel and fend off the occupying Romans and take his rightful place upon the throne of King David—were dashed. Instead of standing at the vanguard of a new period of restored glory, the disciples were given more work to do and a long list of dangerous situations to endure.

This idea—that Jesus represented the hope of restoration of a lost and glorious past—haunts the New Testament. Today, many Christians think of the word *messiah* as an essentially religious term, but it was not so in the first century. *Messiah* literally means "anointed one" in Hebrew, and that anointing refers to the ceremonies by which a king of Israel or Judah would have been inaugurated and installed. It's a term reserved for a political figure. The New Testament calls Jesus *messiah* throughout its pages, or more frequently the Greek equivalent *Christ*, even though Jesus did not look very much like a traditional messianic figure. Instead of evicting the invaders and restoring the kingdom, Jesus was crucified by Rome, and the empire barely noticed his existence as it went about its business of administering and pacifying and taxing a remote province like Judea. Anytime the New Testament calls Jesus the *messiah*, we should read that word with a note of disappointment—as a hope that did not come to pass, at least in the form that some people intended.

But even though Jesus did not end up being the kind of military and political messiah that the disciples were expecting or hoping for, the Book of Acts is full of language and ideas you would expect from people who were hoping for a revolution. The Book of Acts is full of tellings and retellings of Israel's history, in which characters are trying to frame the present and the future in terms of the past. This happens quite a few times in Acts, and one of the most prominent examples comes in chapters 6 and 7, in the story of a man named Stephen.

Stephen, as Acts tells it, was a man "full of grace and power" with a "face like the face of an angel" (6:15), who went around teaching the people. But some people didn't like Stephen's words, and Acts tells the story of how some of those people Stephen offended brought him to the city's ruling council for examination. As part of his defense, Stephen gave a lengthy speech, which takes up almost all of chapter 7. The speech is a recitation of Israel's history, beginning with the story of Abraham and journeying with the patriarchs to the time of Moses and Joshua and ultimately David and Solomon. The endpoint of Stephen's speech was a sharp criticism of the Jerusalem council itself, and of its members, for being complicit in the death of Jesus and for not adequately keeping the Jewish law.

It's important to pause here and remember that this was an internal Jewish dispute. While it can be tempting to read passages like this one as a clash between Christian and Jewish points of view, everyone in this story was Jewish, and their dispute was about the meaning and purpose of Jewish (Israelite) history. There was, at the time this story takes place, no such thing as Christianity, so it was not and could not have been a Jewish/Christian conflict. Instead, this is a window into the ways history can be told and retold to serve the purposes of the present. Stephen was convinced that Jesus was the natural culmination and endpoint of Israel's history—that all the stories beginning with Moses and leading up to David and Solomon had been pointing toward Jesus and his rightful role as Israel's leader. The members of the council, meanwhile, were not so sure. Perhaps they saw themselves as the rightful inheritors of Israel, or perhaps they did not anticipate a restoration of Israel's monarchy the way Stephen seems to have done. In any event, this dispute turned on the question of how the past informs the present and the future, and the telling of history mattered a great deal in the arguments of each side.

Stephen's telling of history mattered so much, in fact, that it cost him his life. After Stephen accused the council of being "betrayers and murderers" of "the Righteous One" (7:52) and accused them of not keeping the law, the council became enraged. Stephen had been very disrespectful to them in his telling of history. He had made them into the villains. They took him out of town and stoned him to death. Stephen is often called the first Christian martyr—the first of the "witnesses" Jesus had promised in 1:8. His dying words, as Acts records them, were a vision of Jesus reigning at the right hand of God. Stephen died secure in his conviction that Jesus stood at the endpoint of a long history of God bringing salvation to Israel—that Jesus was the one Israel had been moving toward all along.

Stephen's speech was one of the first moments of someone appealing to history in Acts, but it wasn't the last. Nor were only Jewish (or Judean) people making those historical appeals. As the Book of Acts follows the apostles across the territories of the Roman Empire, history plays an important role in several dramatic scenes. Everywhere they went, figures like Paul seem to have inspired or provoked the people they met to think about their own people's histories, to talk about the past in nationalistic terms, and to react violently when their vision of history was challenged. Many of the stories found in Acts are about how the presence of Jesus' apostles created anxiety in the people they encountered and how those people began to recite their own histories in response to the claims of the Jesus Movement.

A good example happens in chapter 16 of Acts, which recounts that Paul and Silas ended up in prison in a Roman colonial town called Philippi. At first glance this story, the heart of which appears in 16:16–24 (though it continues through the end of the chapter at verse 40), does not have a whole lot to do with history. But just beneath the surface, history and historical claims drive the narrative. The conflict begins in 16:16 when Paul, Silas, and some unnamed others (including, perhaps, the narrator, since this is one of the Book of Acts' famous "we" passages told in the first-person plural) encounter an enslaved girl. This girl, as the NRSVue and other modern translations put it, had a "spirit of divination" (16:16). The Greek behind it is more complicated, literally reading as "a spirit of the python," and many scholars understand that strange phrase to mean that this enslaved girl was a kind of seer or oracle connected to the cult of Apollo at the famous site of Delphi. In that case, she represented a long and storied tradition of Greek religion and cultural power. And in her case, she represented a lot of economic power too. We know this because the enslaved girl followed Paul and his companions around, announcing that "these men are slaves of the Most High God, who proclaim to you the way of salvation," in verse 17. There is nothing in that statement with which Paul would have disagreed! The girl was telling the truth as Paul and the others would have understood it, which bolsters the possibility that she was somehow connected to the Delphic religious activities that were already centuries old by then. But Paul apparently found her annoying because he cast the spirit out of her.

Paul's actions likely created a terrible crisis for this enslaved girl because—even though she was enslaved—she probably had a bit of status and perhaps even power due to her prophetic abilities. But with those gone, she would have been relegated to far worse fates among the rest of the enslaved people. Acts doesn't tell us anything about how she felt in that moment or what happened to her afterward, but it does tell us how her owners reacted. They were angry. Their ability to profit from the girl had just taken a big hit. We will return to this story a few times later in this book, but for now let's focus on what the enslaved girl's owners said when they brought her to the local Philippian authorities. "These men," they said, "these Jews, are disturbing our city and are advocating customs that are not lawful for us, being Romans, to adopt or observe" (16:20–21).

The slave owners' *grievance*, Acts tells us, had to do with their lost economic power, but when they spoke to the authorities their formal *claims* were not about profit and loss but about custom and peoplehood. Notice how they position Paul and Silas as Jews, or Judeans—people from the province of Judea. This was probably a way to minimize Paul's and Silas' importance and to marginalize them as people, since Judea was a minor and cantankerous province on the edges of the empire. And notice how the slave owners described themselves, placing themselves within the category of "Romans" and the customs proper to Roman people. The slave owners' claim of Roman-ness wasn't accidental, and it wasn't casual. As a Roman colony in Greece, Philippi would have understood itself as a special outpost of Roman identity. Although the Roman Empire stretched as far as the eye could see, most of the empire was made up of subjected territories and peoples. Philippi, however, was a Roman colony, settled by retired military veterans, and it probably clung very tightly to its status as especially Roman. By contrasting Paul and Silas to themselves in terms of peoplehood and belonging, the slave owners were appealing to Roman custom and history to justify their actions in the present and to argue for a certain kind of future. In their minds, this was a future in which Paul and Silas would be punished as the meddling outsiders they were. Interestingly, only a dozen or so verses later Acts drops a bombshell. "They have beaten us in public," Paul said to the man who was charged with jailing him and Silas, "uncondemned, men who are Romans, and have thrown us into prison, and now they are going to discharge us in secret?" (16:37). Suddenly, after being treated like outsiders, Paul claimed that he and Silas were "Romans," that is, citizens and insiders just like the slave owners had been claiming to be. Whether that was true is an interesting historical question; scholars are divided on the question of whether Paul would have held citizenship. But it was true enough, in the moment, that Paul and Silas got an apology from the magistrates and regained their freedom. Paul, it seems, was a kind of shapeshifter who could finesse his identity to suit all kinds of new circumstances and purposes.

In the very next chapter, as Paul and Silas visited the northern Greek city of Thessalonica, not far from Philippi, history played an important role once more. In that city, Acts describes the apostles visiting a Jewish synagogue, where they preached that the Jewish messiah—which, again, most Jews at that time would have understood to have been a military or political leader—would need "to suffer and to rise from the dead" (17:3). In response to their preaching, some Jews were convinced and others were outraged by the idea that a messiah might die and rise again. This was common pattern in Acts' storytelling—acceptance on the part of some who heard the apostles' message and incredulity on the part of others. In Thessalonica, the conflict exploded into a full-on riot, and the rioters seized a man named Jason, whom they accused of hosting Paul and Silas. "These people who have been turning the world upside down have come here also," the mob told the authorities, "and Jason has entertained them as guests." That accusation—that the apostles had been turning the world upside down—was a way of saying that Paul and Silas were upending the ideas of history and belonging that bound the Roman Empire together. "They are all acting contrary to the decrees of the emperor," the Thessalonians said, and then most critically, "saying that there is another king named Jesus" (17:7). In other words, the residents of Thessalonica had taken at face value Paul and Silas' preaching in the synagogue that Jesus was the messiah, and they had concluded—rightly—that Paul and Silas were loyal to a different king than Caesar. While a lot of nuance was lost in that exchange (Paul probably would have wanted to emphasize that Jesus was a different sort of king than Caesar, and the Book of Acts itself would want to reiterate that it was telling the story not of a political revolution but of a religious movement), the substance of the charge was true enough. Paul and Silas had been pushing a different kind of history, and a different vision for the future, than the one sanctioned by the empire.

I'll give one more example to make the point. In chapter 19 of Acts, a couple of years or more after the events in Thessalonica, Paul found himself in Ephesus, which was an enormous and prosperous city on the west coast of Asia Minor, in what is now Turkey. Ephesus was known for its massive temple to the goddess Artemis, which was an important site of worship, pilgrimage, and tourism and which was considered one of the seven wonders of the ancient world. The conflict in chapter 19 came when a group of silversmiths—people who made religious goods to sell to the people who came to visit the temple—noticed that Paul's preaching had put a dent in their business. A prominent silversmith named Demetrius rallied the others, and he did it using an appeal to history and to the cultural power of the city itself. Speaking to them (in 19:27), Demetrius said that "there is danger not only that this trade of ours may come into disrepute but also that the temple of the great goddess Artemis will be scorned, and she will be deprived of her majesty that brought all Asia and the world to worship her." Demetrius was making an argument about the city's identity as it was rooted in its traditions and history. The artisans' response was to shout "Great is Artemis of the Ephesians," and with this patriotic refrain they gathered a crowd to themselves, and eventually a mob.

We will revisit this story later as an example of economic protectionism, but for now, notice how the silversmiths made claims to the city's past and its reputation as a cultic site for Artemis. *Yes, we will lose our livelihoods*, the men were saying, *but more than that, our city will lose its essence*. There's a bit of Make Ephesus Great Again to their shouts of "Great Is Artemis of the Ephesians"—a claim that only by staying faithful to the past and by maintaining bygone glory could the city prosper. The Ephesians were fearful and angry that their city and its traditions would be degraded by the influence of outsiders, just like the Philippians were and just like the members of the council in Jerusalem were. Like the people in those other cities, the Ephesians reacted with violence and by appealing to history—by pointing to the ways their city's identity was rooted in the past and must be maintained into the future.

All these examples from Acts point to the ways the characters in the book use history to imagine the future, how they leverage the past to create belonging in the present, and how they draw lines of inclusion and exclusion based on their visions of historical events. In Jerusalem, Stephen's speech recited Israel's history as a way to establish what he thought should be its future. In Philippi, Paul's actions toward the enslaved girl who was connected to Delphi ended up ensnaring him in a debate about Romanness. In Thessalonica, Paul's preaching about Jesus as messiah raised alarms among the city's residents, who noticed how Paul's worldview came from a different historical perspective that might be threatening to the Roman Empire. And in Ephesus, the city's history was so powerful as a starting point for understanding its present and its future that it made Paul seem threatening enough to incite a riot. In a giant system like the Roman Empire, with its rich and dominant narratives about the past and with the ways the empire derived its power from its traditions, the actions of Paul, Silas, Stephen, and others felt threatening to the people they met—threatening enough to inspire violence and conflict everywhere they went.

Living with Historical Narratives

As a kid growing up in the South, I learned the power of historical narratives to shape how people see the world. Even when those narratives were mostly unspoken—even when they showed up in subtle things like the names of places and the inscriptions on monuments—history was a powerful force that influenced how I saw the world. The people who could impose their view of history on everyone else had a huge advantage as they attempted to spread their ideas.

In many ways, the Book of Acts attempts to do exactly that: it attempts to impose a certain view of history on its readers. Acts understands that Jesus is Lord and that Israel's history had been leading up to a figure like Jesus who was a messiah who would be raised from the dead. Acts wants to tell its story so that the reader comes to believe those things are true. And as Acts tells its story, it encounters other stories, each vying to influence people: the stories of the members of the Jerusalem council, the stories found in Philippi and Thessalonica and Ephesus, and others along the way. As an author, Luke was quite aware of the power gained by leveraging history, and he paid close attention to history's influence as he told his story.

In our own world today, history remains a powerful tool for imposing and leveraging worldviews. All around the United States, school boards have fought over textbooks because they understand that how history is taught makes a difference in how people understand themselves and the world around them. The Trump Administration has been restoring old names and reinstalling old statues because—in the words of Trump's executive order—he thought that removing the statues was "undermining the remarkable achievements of the United States by casting its founding principles and historical milestones in a negative light." When you want to Make America Great Again, the past can never be cast in a "negative light" because the past is the place to which the nation should want to return. So the past itself becomes a battleground—the place where control over the future is decided.

When living under an autocratic system—the kind of system that wants to control historical narratives to control people's ideas about themselves—there are a few ways you can resist. Probably the most important form of resistance is to insist on and protect quality education and information, from preschool to higher education, and from social media to public media like NPR and PBS. Because they understand the power of knowledge to undermine bad historical narratives, autocrats and authoritarians often attack the free press and manipulate social media, and they limit access to education or attempt to control it and bend it to their purposes. If people aren't offered access to an education that builds critical thinking skills and exposes them to a variety of viewpoints and historical sources, they will be susceptible to their leaders' manipulation.

Beyond that, one of the most effective forms of resistance is simply a healthy curiosity about one's own place in the world. For some people, this could look like skepticism—it could involve asking questions about the supposed greatness of one's nation or group. For others, the curiosity could be softer—a genuine interest in how other people understand themselves and organize their lives. This curiosity could begin with noticing that lots of different people live in lots of different ways and that one's own traditions and histories are not the only possibilities, and indeed that they might not always be the best.

That's what happened to me after I moved away from the South. Living elsewhere, I began to notice how narrow my education had been and how limited my exposure had been to different kinds of people. I began to learn to see others as they see themselves and to see myself as others might see me. This didn't lead me to reject the land or the people where I was raised: quite the contrary. It led me to appreciate my place in the world more, to criticize it when it needs criticizing and to praise it where it deserves praise, and to recognize how my own position in the world has shaped who I am. Living through times like these, such actions as understanding oneself, understanding others, and recognizing the power of history can be revolutionary.

Further Reading

This chapter involves discussion of some of the most interesting parts of Acts, and there are fascinating resources out there for anyone interested in doing some more reading. If you are curious about the story of Stephen and how it shaped and was shaped by the patterns of Christian martyrdom narratives, then Shelly Matthews' book *Perfect Martyr* will hold a lot of interest for you.[2] And if you are interested in martyrdom more broadly (not necessarily

[2] Shelly Matthews, *Perfect Martyr: The Stoning of Stephen and the Construction of Christian Identity* (Oxford University Press, 2010).

connected to the Book of Acts), Candida Moss' book *The Myth of Persecution* is a great starting point.[3]

The story of the enslaved girl in Acts 16 is fascinating, and recent years have seen a wave of great scholarship on this passage specifically and on slavery in the ancient world in general. Mitzi Smith's work has long brought attention to the ways slavery functions in the New Testament and to how slavery in the New Testament helped to justify and authorize modern forms of slavery.[4] Jennifer Glancy was a pioneer in this area, and her work remains indispensable.[5] Katherine Shaner's work focuses specifically on how enslaved people took leadership positions within early Christian traditions and what the implications of that might be.[6] My colleague Christy Cobb has written extensively on slavery and early Christianity, including her book *Slavery, Gender, Truth, and Power in Luke-Acts and Other Ancient Narratives*,[7] and just recently Cobb and Shaner coedited a fantastic volume titled *Ancient Slavery and Its New Testament Contexts.* Finally, another Candida Moss book, *God's Ghostwriters*, explores the relationship between the New Testament itself and the enslaved people who were responsible for writing much of it.[8]

---

[3] Candida Moss, *The Myth of Persecution: How Early Christians Invented a Story of Martyrdom* (HarperOne, 2013).

[4] A good starting point is Mitzi Smith, "Slavery and the Early Church," in *True to Our Native Land: An African American New Testament Commentary*, ed. Brian K. Blount et al. (Fortress Press, 2007).

[5] Jennifer Glancy, *Slavery in Early Christianity* (Oxford University Press, 2002).

[6] Katherine A. Shaner, *Enslaved Leadership in Early Christianity* (Oxford University Press, 2018).

[7] Christy Cobb, *Slavery, Gender, Truth, and Power in Luke-Acts and Other Ancient Narratives* (Palgrave Macmillan, 2019).

[8] Candida Moss, *God's Ghostwriters: Enslaved Christians and the Making of the Bible* (Little, Brown and Company, 2024).

3

Territory

I have always wanted to travel to Greenland, but I have never had the chance. Greenland ticks all the boxes for a place I would love to visit. The island is wildly natural and generally unspoiled, capped with ice and filled with wildlife. Its mountains rise dramatically above the slow-flowing ice of glaciers, and the waters off its coasts teem with whales and seals. Each time I see Greenland in a film or television show, my desire to travel there is renewed.

Lately, Greenland has been in the news because President Donald Trump has been musing about acquiring it for the United States. Although the island is not for sale and its national leaders in Greenland and in Denmark (where the government still helps administer Greenland) have insisted that it never *will be* for sale, Trump has persisted in floating it as a possibility. He has even hinted that if he can't buy Greenland, he might simply take it by force. (He has said similar things about the Panama Canal, and between the time when I finished this book manuscript and when the copyediting was finished, Trump had ordered the capture of Venezuela's president Nicolás Maduro and the effective seizure of its oil resources.) An island like Greenland is strategically positioned to be very important as climate change reshapes the world, and possession of Greenland would allow the United States to project power deep into the Arctic Circle (useful both for stationing armed forces and for refueling war machinery) and to mine the island for its rare earth resources.

Although many people and countries have mocked Trump for his comments, he's actually on very familiar territory, historically speaking. The history of the world's empires—and the history of the leaders of those empires—is full of land grabs just like this one. That's what empires do, really: they seize territory, one way or another, or they otherwise bring it under their control. Then empires use those territories to build out the systems by which they prosper at others' expense.

When I was a teen at summer camp, a counselor came into the cabin one evening with a grave look on his face. He sat us all down—a bunch of thirteen-year-old boys—and told us that Iraq had invaded Kuwait. It didn't mean a lot to me at the time, though I could tell the news had really shaken the counselor. At that very moment, he told us, Iraqi troops were rolling into Kuwait and seizing its oil fields; and the counselor said Iraq's leader—Saddam Hussein—coveted Kuwait's wealth in oil reserves. I could not have pointed to either country on a map that day, but all the grown-ups seemed to think it was a very serious situation. A few months later, the United States and a coalition of other countries invaded Iraq and freed Kuwait from Iraqi control. The war was shockingly quick and violent, and at the time it was remarkable in that it was fought substantially from the air. I can remember the surge of patriotism in my small hometown, including a pro-war parade full of waving American flags. I can also remember hearing people make accusations, faintly and around the edges at first and more loudly later, that Desert Storm (as the operation was called) was not a war about principles or freedom or protecting the innocent but a war over control of oil.

Soon I was in high school, and questions about the Gulf War lingered like the American troops that were still stationed in the Middle East in huge numbers. (My father would later spend three months in Saudi Arabia as an Air Force reservist.) There was no question that Iraq's invasion of Kuwait had its origins at least partly in disputes over oil. Iraq's earlier criticism of Kuwait exceeding its OPEC quotas contributed to the hostility between the two nations leading up to the invasion. And the United States' appetite for oil had always been a major driver of the world's oil markets. Soon some of my high school classmates and even some teachers began to suggest that the United States' participation in the war was not strictly altruistic, aimed at defending a smaller nation, but that it was carried out to secure a steady supply of inexpensive oil. I wasn't sure what to think.

Now, as an adult who studies and teaches history, I have learned that imperial systems tend to follow patterns. If you zoom out from the details of any particular conflict or war, and if you pay attention to the actions empires have tended to take across time and space, you can see that the Gulf War—and Trump's open musings about buying or taking Greenland by force—fit into a familiar pattern. So, too, do many other conflicts in the world today and many of the wars we study in history classes. To understand these patterns and what they have to do with empires and the people who lead them, let's turn to an overview of the relationships between empires and territory.

How Do Empires and Autocrats Think about Territory?

Empires *eat* territory—that's the first thing to know. Territory is how empires grow, move, and reproduce. Territory is the fuel that keeps empires going. So territory is always the first concern of any empire's leader.

Empires take many forms, and the ways they consume territory can vary a lot from one to the next. If we think back to some of history's earliest empires like Akkad, Egypt, Babylon, and Carthage, we see them expanding voraciously across territory—defeating their neighbors in battle then either annexing them into the empire or setting them up as vassal states obligated to pay tribute. Different empires had different strategies for this, and all those strategies had their pluses and minuses. Direct administration of a territory was most straightforward, but it could be complicated by cultural differences and the constant threat of rebellion, and it required a lot of resources. Many empires preferred to leave their conquered territories intact but to lace them together with the empire with a common language, cultural system, or set of financial incentives. No matter which method an empire used, the key was to accomplish at least two things: first, empires want to harvest the maximum revenue and goods from their territories while putting the minimum of investment possible into maintaining control. Second, empires often seek to control territories in order to put a buffer between themselves and their enemies, to boost security for the center by confining conflict and violence to the peripheries. Let's talk about these two patterns.

First, let's discuss resources. Empires, generally speaking, pull resources from their peripheries to enrich their centers. Whether the peripheral territories are part of the empire proper or client states run by puppet rulers, the goal of the empire is the same: squeeze out all the wealth they can and bring it to the people and the institutions at the center of the empire. A good example of this is what happened in Ukraine during Russia's invasion. As we discussed in the previous chapter, Vladimir Putin said outright that Russia invaded Ukraine because he believed (as many Russians do) that Ukraine is rightly part of a unified greater Russia and that Ukraine's belonging to the old Russian and Soviet empires means it should also belong to a twenty-first-century Russia. But many observers have noted Ukraine's value lies not only in its cultural and historical significance but also in its territory, which is rich in natural resources. Ukraine holds some of the world's best agricultural land and is often called the breadbasket of Europe. So right away Ukraine is valuable for that reason. But Ukraine also holds vast resources in rare earth minerals, which are critical (and in short supply) for emerging technologies like electronics and the batteries used in electric vehicles. Many political skirmishes around the world actually are struggles over these kinds of resources, and many observers think Russia invaded Ukraine partly to seize control of its mineral deposits. The United States confirmed that, in a way, when it made rare earth minerals a part of its negotiations with Ukraine. The Trump Administration has offered Ukraine some of the security guarantees it seeks as part of a deal to end the war with

Russia, on the condition that the United States will have access to Ukraine's mineral wealth. In that sense, the conflict in Ukraine is really a conflict between two world powers and their leaders, both of which are squabbling over the resources of the same less powerful nation—not so different from Iraq and the United States fighting each other over who would have access to Kuwait's oil.

The ancient world was full of these same kinds of conflicts over resource extraction, and ancient empires also were motivated to conquer and control territory to guarantee access to certain supplies. Egypt, for example, was its own kind of ancient breadbasket, producing massive amounts of grain. The Roman Empire, therefore, sought to subjugate and control Egypt, and it used its military power against Egypt to ensure that the people back in Italy had enough to eat. On the other end of the Roman Empire in Spain, ingenious Roman engineers went so far as to reroute rivers, sending them through mountains to hollow them out to gain access to the metal deposits inside. This form of hydraulic mining was environmentally catastrophic and often deadly for the enslaved people who worked the mines, but a huge empire like Rome needed access to the deposits of gold found in the mountains, even if that meant destroying many lives and faraway landscapes to get it.

Perhaps the best example of resource extraction, though, and certainly the most widespread, was taxation. When an empire like Rome conquered a territory, the people in that territory became *subjects* of the empire, but they normally did not become *citizens*. That is, the conquered people did not necessarily gain any rights or even much security, but they did become obligated to support the empire in various ways. One of the most important of those means of supporting the empire was taxes. The New Testament is full of references to taxes and tax collectors, which tells us that the people of Judea (which was a province of Rome that had been conquered relatively recently) could feel very strongly the presence of Rome's tax system. Often, tax collectors are lumped together in the gospels with various kinds of socially undesirable people, as in Luke 18:11, where we read about a Pharisee giving thanks to God that he is "not like other people: thieves, rogues, adulterers, or even like this tax collector." Throughout the gospels, tax collectors get this kind of treatment: they are described in broadly suspicious and vaguely sinful terms. This was because of the ways tax collectors did the dirty work of the Roman Empire. A province like Judea was squeezed mercilessly for tax revenue, and the goods collected as taxes (like wine and olive oil) and money paid in taxes flowed from Judea on the empire's periphery into Rome at the empire's center.

The second function of territory for empires is to serve as a buffer between them and their enemies. This is a major part of why President Trump is interested in Greenland: strategically, it's an important piece of land as polar ice caps melt and open up sea routes that might connect North America to Asia and Europe more quickly. Greenland would serve as a very good buffer. The idea of a land buffer is also an important aspect of the conflict in Ukraine. Europe sees Ukraine as a buffer between itself and Russia, and Russia has always been insistent that Ukraine—whatever form it ends up taking—could never be part of an organization like NATO because that would bring the influence of Europe too close to Russia's borders. Both Europe and Russia understand Ukraine as a kind of buffer against the other.

In the ancient world, empires thought the same way. The united kingdom of Israel—and later the two divided kingdoms, the northern kingdom of Israel and the southern kingdom of Judah—sometimes served this purpose for their neighbors in the region. Powerful and aggressive empires surrounded Israel: Assyria to the north, Egypt to the south, and Babylon and Persia to the east. Israel happened to occupy one of the most convenient strips of land in the region, if you were one of those huge empires and you were wanting to march an army through. So the history of Israel was full of threats and violence from those big empires, which were all trying to use Israel and Judah as buffers and staging areas for their attacks on each other. For small nations like Israel and Judah, sovereignty could only be found rarely and briefly. Most of their time was spent managing relationships with much more powerful empires and trying to carve out an existence in the margins between them.

In the period of the New Testament, the province of Judea (which was more or less the ancient kingdom of Judah, having passed through centuries of control by the empires of the Babylonians, the Persians, the Greeks, and finally the Romans) found itself in this same kind of buffer role. Judea was on the far eastern edge of the Roman Empire. Strategically, Judea functioned for Rome much as Greenland would function for the United States, in the unlikely event that President Trump gets his way. Judea was a buffer on the periphery—a militarized zone of protection that kept Rome's enemies to the east at bay. Those eastern enemies were the Parthians, who were centered in what's now Iran and who—like Rome—had their own territorial ambitions. Judea (and other eastern provinces like Syria and, later, Arabia Petraea) helped Rome put the brakes on any potential invasion. Because it was acting as a buffer—and because provinces at the peripheries tended to be a bit more difficult to control than the ones closer to the center—the region hosted large standing armies of Roman soldiers. Those soldiers, organized into legions, were there to pacify the Judeans and Syrians in their eastern provinces. But the soldiers were also there to deter the Parthians from getting any notions of invading. During Jesus' lifetime, Rome didn't station any legions in Judea itself, but there was always one stationed in Syria, just to the north, and the pages of the gospels are full of references to Roman soldiers, centurions, tribunes, cohorts, and even legions.

Later, during the period in which the Book of Acts was written, a cataclysmic war changed Rome's calculations and brought two legions to Judea itself. In the years 66 to 70 C.E., the residents of Judea rebelled against Rome in the Jewish War. The Jewish War proved to be difficult for Rome to subdue, and it was a bit bruising to the imperial ego. But ultimately the Roman Empire prevailed, and Judea—and especially Jerusalem—was broadly razed. According to Josephus (whose accounts always need an asterisk beside them because of questions about his reliability and allegiances), over a million Jews died in the war. Historians might dispute those figures, but there is no question that by the time the Book of Acts was written the province of Judea was haunted by an immense presence of imperial violence, and it had been reminded forcefully of its place as a puppet of the Roman state. Rome sent two legions to Judea following the war: the Legio X Fretensis, which was based near the ruins of Jerusalem itself, and later the Legio VI Ferrata (an "iron" legion), which was stationed in the north. By the time Acts was written, the military occupation of Judea had intensified and anyone living or traveling in Judea or Jerusalem would have encountered constant reminders of Roman power and presence.

Both of these patterns for acquiring and using territory—resource extraction and using the periphery as a buffer against external enemies—persist from the ancient world to the present. They help us understand the logic of empires and the thinking of the people who lead them. We can see those patterns unfolding in the world today in conflicts and potential conflicts in places as far-flung as Congo, Taiwan, Mexico, Ukraine, and Greenland. And we can see those same patterns as they influence the story Acts tells. Let's turn to some of the places in Acts where we can see those patterns in action.

Territory in Acts

A defining feature of Acts is its geographical vision. More than any other book of the New Testament, the Book of Acts is preoccupied with territory. If you remember that opening question of Acts that we talked about in the last chapter, you'll see this in action. "Lord, is this the time when you will restore the kingdom to Israel?" the apostles asked Jesus in 1:6. Jesus' response was essentially to say no, but it was also more complicated than that. "But you will receive power when the Holy Spirit has come upon you," Jesus says in 1:8, "and you will be my witnesses in Jerusalem, in all Judea and Samaria, and to the ends of the earth." This is a theological agenda; Jesus anticipates that the work of the Holy Spirit will govern the apostles' lives. But it is also a territorial agenda. Beginning from Jerusalem, where they were gathered, the apostles would be sent "to the ends of the earth." The kingdom might not be restored to Israel right away, but Acts promised that the power and the presence of the God of Israel would spread to the ends of the earth.

Of course, the earth is a sphere and does not have "ends," but if we put ourselves into the mindset of Jesus and the apostles, the phrase makes a lot of sense. Already by the first century the work of scientists and the observations of seafaring traders had popularized the notion that the earth was round, but the portion of the earth that could be known by any single person was somewhat limited. To the east, the campaigns of Alexander the Great several centuries earlier had connected the Mediterranean world to the Indian subcontinent, and ancient maps and written sources provide evidence of Greek and Roman influence as far east as Sri Lanka. Meanwhile, the Parthian Empire to Rome's east controlled trade along the Silk Road, which was already sufficiently robust and established that goods could flow freely between China and western Europe. To the west, the known world ended in Spain and Britain, which were both under Roman control in the first century. To the south, the Roman Empire had provinces across North Africa and knowledge of and relationships with other kingdoms and empires deep into the continent's interior. And around the time of the New Testament the Roman Empire was attempting—ultimately without much success—to push its boundaries into northern Europe. Even though people knew the earth was round, the *known* world—the world that was conceivable given the knowledge they had at the time—had ends.

The Book of Acts is very interested in those ends. In some ways, the Book of Acts pushes back against the Roman Empire and resists seeing the world the way the empire's autocratic leaders would have seen it. Acts is saying no to the territorial logics of empire. But in other ways, Acts accepts the Roman Empire's boundaries as the "ends of the earth," and it reproduces those boundaries in the ways it thinks about territory—the ways it tells the stories of the apostles' travels "to the ends of the earth." A quick tour of the Book of Acts shows this to be the case.

Not long after Jesus promised the arrival of the Holy Spirit in 1:6–8, that promise came true. In chapter 2—one of the most famous passages from the Book of Acts—the apostles are gathered together in Jerusalem for the Pentecost festival when the Holy Spirit arrives in dramatic fashion. Most churches today still celebrate Pentecost, so you might be familiar with the story. I want to focus on just one part of the passage, which is the part that has made many a liturgist wish they had not signed up to read scripture on Pentecost: Acts 2:5–13. Here, Luke describes the crowd in Jerusalem for Pentecost and the crowd's reaction to the way Jesus' disciples suddenly have the ability to speak in foreign languages:

> Now there were devout Jews from every people under heaven living in Jerusalem. And at this sound the crowd gathered and was bewildered,

> because each one heard them speaking in the native language of each. Amazed and astonished, they asked, "Are not all these who are speaking Galileans? And how is it that we hear, each of us, in our own native language? Parthians, Medes, Elamites, and residents of Mesopotamia, Judea and Cappadocia, Pontus and Asia, Phrygia and Pamphylia, Egypt and the parts of Libya belonging to Cyrene, and visitors from Rome, both Jews and proselytes, Cretans and Arabs—in our own languages we hear them speaking about God's deeds of power." All were amazed and perplexed, saying to one another, "What does this mean?" But others sneered and said, "They are filled with new wine."

The list of territories here is dizzying and probably terrifying if you have been charged with reading this passage out loud on a Sunday morning. You likely recognize some of the names of places—Egypt and Libya, for example, and Parthia, which we have already been discussing. But other territories are more obscure. Who still knows where Phrygia and Pamphylia are—let alone how to pronounce them? Surely this passage would have been just as effective if Luke had stopped after writing "Now there were devout Jews from every people under heaven living in Jerusalem" and not proceeded to enumerate a list of them. Everyone would have gotten the idea. So why does Luke go to the trouble to list them?

In this list of places, Luke reiterates—and expands on—the short list found in 1:8. There, Jesus told the apostles they would be "witnesses in Jerusalem, in all Judea and Samaria, and to the ends of the earth," but here in chapter 2 Luke spells that out a little more fully by name-checking places from all over the empire, from its peripheries to its center in Rome itself, from south to north and east to west. In this way, Luke imagines the spread of the Jesus Movement, and he does it using the categories provided by the Roman Empire itself. The places named in this passage range from Parthia in the east (modern-day Iran) to Media and Elam (modern-day Iraq, roughly), to several locations in Asia Minor (modern-day Turkey—Pontus, Cappadocia, Phrygia, Pamphylia, Asia), to North Africa (Egypt and Libya), to the island of Crete in the middle of the Mediterranean Sea, to Rome in Italy.

Even though Acts tells a story that's critical of the Roman Empire in many ways, it uses the logic of the Roman Empire to organize and think about territory in telling the story. That turns out to be true of the Book of Acts as a whole, not just this passage. The story of Acts unfolds from east to west, first in Judea and Samaria, then to Asia Minor, Greece, and finally Italy, where Acts concludes its narrative with Paul under house arrest in Rome. Luke's literary territorial imagination is very much like the Roman imperial territorial imagination in that it envisions the Jesus Movement traveling on imperial roads to imperial cities and colonies and finally to the imperial capital. But perhaps most interestingly Acts tells its story in the same direction as the Roman Empire drew resources from the people: from the periphery to the center. Acts' story begins in the imperial hinterlands, all the way on the eastern edge of the empire. But it concludes at the center, to which the Roman Empire had been extracting the revenues and resources from Judea for decades.

One interesting aspect of this flow from east to west in Acts is that the narrative travels along diaspora networks. We briefly discussed diaspora a couple of chapters ago, but it's worth pausing here to understand it better. Although Jews were Judeans (the word in Greek is the same for both of those English words), many Jews lived outside of Judea, all around the Roman Empire and even outside of it. Scholars call this the *diaspora*, which means "dispersion" in the sense of a scattering (like seeds), and the diaspora existed because of past examples of imperial violence that caused the people to scatter, much as refugees do today. Following invasions of the northern kingdom of Israel by the Assyrians and especially following the invasion of the southern kingdom of Judah by the Babylonians, people from Israel and Judah moved across the Mediterranean. They also moved for other reasons—to seek economic opportunity, for example, or because they had been captured and enslaved and shipped to distant lands. By the time of the events in the Book of Acts, there were Jewish populations in many of the cities of the Roman Empire. As Acts tells its story—especially the story of Paul's journeys west—it often uses diasporic synagogues and Jewish communities as waypoints along the journey. In that way, Acts describes an incursion of a Judean movement into Roman space, but it's doing so by tracing the histories of violence and disruption that empire itself had brought about.

Paul was a diaspora Jew, hailing from Tarsus in the Roman province of Cilicia. So were many of the other figures in Acts, including both the Jesus Movement's allies and many of its opponents. It was diaspora Jews who helped rile up the council that stoned Stephen to death in chapter 7, for example, and it was diaspora Jews who attacked Paul in the temple in chapter 21. Many modern Christians read these stories—wrongly, in my opinion—as stories of how Jews were hostile to Christians. In fact, we shouldn't read these as stories about Jews and Christians at all, since at that point there was nothing called Christianity yet. Instead, we should think of these stories as conflicts between different groups of Jews. In these cases, and in a few other cases in Acts, the conflicts arose because of differences of opinions between Judean Jews (Jews living in Judea and especially in Jerusalem) and diaspora Jews (Jews living elsewhere in the Roman Empire). The way Acts tells the story of the Jesus Movement emphasizes the role of territory—how the empire itself had disrupted Judean-ness and Jewishness and scattered people all over. Acts also emphasizes the same dynamics of center and periphery that the Roman Empire did, although Acts flips the dynamic. Instead of taking resources from the periphery to serve the center or counting on the periphery to act like a buffer against external enemies, Acts narrates what happens when the periphery begins to encroach on the center and when the people from the edges of empire begin to make their way toward its heart.

One story that plays with this dynamic of center and periphery comes in the latter part of Acts 8. It's a strange story in many ways, featuring a scene that has an odd relationship to place and territory. In it, the apostle Philip was visited by an angel who told him to travel to a road connecting Jerusalem to Gaza (which was a southward route toward Egypt). The road, Acts tells us, goes through the wilderness. Along the way, Philip saw a person, whom Acts describes with a bevy of identity markers. This person was an Ethiopian, a court official who served as treasurer for the Candace (the queen of the Ethiopians), a pilgrim to Jerusalem, a literate person who was reading a scroll of the prophet Isaiah, and a eunuch. These various identities overlap in ways that help us make some sense of them. Eunuchs (most often, people who had been castrated as boys, which was thought to render them more useful for imperial service) did often work for important political figures. They could reach positions of great power and responsibility, as this person seems to have done.

There are a few curious things about this particular person. First, the Ethiopian seems to have been enamored of Jerusalem, the prophet Isaiah, and perhaps Judea itself. Scholars have pointed to a number of possibilities here. Some see the eunuch as a curious seeker who took the opportunity on a work trip to explore a new religious identity. Others see the eunuch as a Judean in exile—a diaspora Jew—who had returned home. Perhaps the eunuch was, or had been, enslaved, and was rekindling the broken connection with a lost homeland and people. But the second really curious thing is that this eunuch was Ethiopian. Ethiopia was a long way from Judea—far on the other side of Egypt, outside the realm of the Roman Empire. Why is this story in the Book of Acts?

Many scholars see this story about the Ethiopian eunuch as Acts' attempt to transcend the boundaries and confines of the Roman Empire and to fulfill Jesus' promise that the apostles would carry the message about Jesus "to the ends of the earth." Ethiopia certainly would qualify. The Roman world knew about Africa beyond its North African provinces, to be sure. It even traded with the nations and kingdoms there and had diplomatic relations with them. But in a cultural and symbolic sense, the Ethiopian eunuch powerfully shows how the message of the Jesus Movement was traveling well beyond the boundaries of the Roman Empire. Presumably the Ethiopian—whom Philip baptized in a pool of water that had miraculously appeared there in the desert—went back to Ethiopia to spread the word about Jesus further.

The most significant journey in Acts, though, is probably not the eunuch's journey back to Ethiopia. Instead, it is Paul's journey to Rome. Rome was a symbolically important place as the capital of the empire and the seat of imperial power and control. But it was also an incredibly important place culturally and economically—the largest city in the world at the time. In his letter to the Romans (especially in chapter 15), Paul talks about his desire to travel there, though he makes it clear that there were already at least a few thriving communities of Jesus-followers in the city (which he mentions in Romans 16). The way Acts tells it, Paul did finally get his wish to go to Rome, though it was not under the circumstances he might have chosen. Paul, in chapter 25 of Acts, appealed his case to the emperor himself. (More on this in chapter 5 of this book.) Acts chapters 27 and 28, then, detail Paul's journey to Rome as a prisoner, and the book ends with his detention there under house arrest, awaiting his trial. Much ink has been spilled about the ending of Acts. The book kind of fizzles out with Paul in Rome, and it offers little resolution to its long-standing drama. Did Paul get an audience with the emperor? Was he set free? Was he executed? As I said earlier, I suspect that Paul was killed in Rome, but if so, why didn't Luke tell us about it?

That omission—and the rest of Luke's silence about Paul's fate in Rome—makes some sense if we view the Book of Acts in terms of territory. If you think about the big arc of the Book of Acts in terms of territory and geography, and if you think about the ideology of the Roman Empire that Acts itself was trying to undercut in subtle ways, then what better way to end the book than by having one of its chief protagonists—the one whose story the narrative had been following for nearly twenty chapters—finish his story in the most central location of all? The ending of Acts has Paul holding forth, teaching groups of Jewish leaders in the city, very much alive and well. "He lived there two whole years at his own expense," Acts 28:30–31 tells us, "and welcomed all who came to him, proclaiming the kingdom of God and teaching about the Lord Jesus Christ with all boldness and without hindrance." What happened after those "two whole years"? It doesn't seem to have mattered! What mattered, to Luke, was that Paul brought Acts' territorial story to a tidy resting point. The movement from the hinterlands had made its way into the empire's heart.

Living in Empire's Territory

I live in the United States, and based on the distribution profile of this book's publisher, you probably do too. That means we both live in the heart of an empire. Perhaps, like me, you have been in a process of discovering this fact throughout your life, or perhaps you have always understood it or have only just learned it. But however we learn about our place within empire, we have to choose how to live based on what we know.

It's tempting to view the comments of President Trump regarding Greenland (and Panama's canal and Venezuela's oil fields) as some kind of exception or egregious departure from norms. But all that's new about Trump's thirst for Greenland is that he talked about it out loud. For all of my adult life, and before that too, the United States has been behaving as an imperial power behaves, and its leaders have been trying to control territories to leverage them for security and to extract their resources. The wars in the Middle East, the Cold War and the Space Race, the stark policies of presidents like Theodore Roosevelt, the Louisiana Purchase, the ongoing second-class citizenship of Puerto Ricans, the idea of manifest destiny, the establishment of the first European settlements and colonies in North America—they are all expressions of imperial territorial thinking. We live, and have always lived, in the heart of an imperial system. Knowing that, what is the best way to live?

The Book of Acts tells the story of the origins of the tradition we now call Christianity, and it's a story told as a form of resistance to imperial territorial politics. Luke could have written the story of Acts in many ways, and the resurrected Jesus could have framed the apostles' mission in Acts 1:6–8 in many ways. Luke and Jesus chose to tell the story of Christianity as a story about imperial greed for land and territory and the ways in which the Jesus Movement slowly infiltrated the empire's territory and undermined its claims to power. Jesus and Acts could have emphasized theology or the rules for living in religious community, or they could have talked about the Christian tradition as an unfolding of truth into the world. And the story does follow those threads a bit. But overwhelmingly, the story Acts tells is of how some nobodies from the eastern provinces followed God's calling into the heart of empire until one of them was in the capital city, preaching about Jesus.

For those of us who already live in the capital of empire, I think our task is to resist the ideologies of empire and to speak out against the seizure and exploitation of territory (and the people who live in those territories). That sometimes means opposing wars or naked resource grabs like the ones underway in Ukraine and Greenland. But it also means noticing all the other ways we conquer and seize and exploit—like unfair trade policies that bring cheap goods to U.S. consumers while requiring people elsewhere to accept poverty wages and environmental destruction. It might also mean faith communities lending moral support to peacemaking efforts and recognizing the many instances in which the church has been a part of colonizing and imperial programs. It means opposing our leaders—whether they are the ones for whom we voted or not—when they perpetuate or initiate policies that export violence around the world in order to insulate Americans from conflict. And it means listening to the voices of people from the world's edges and from the margins of the United States' own cultural and religious systems—and paying attention to what they tell us. That is, after all, the story the Book of Acts tells. We will look more closely at how that works in the next chapter.

Further Reading

An early and enduringly important article about the role of territory and the Book of Acts—especially as it relates to the story of the Ethiopian eunuch—came from Clarice Martin. In a 1989 article, Martin pointed out the many biases inherent in how the story of the Ethiopian eunuch was studied and how Africa in particular showed up in biblical scholarship.[1] Since then, many others have contributed important work that attends to questions of territory, identity, and the biases inherent in how we read the Bible. Musa Dube reads the story from a migrant's perspective,[2] Manuel Villalobos thinks about territory and identity,[3] and Sean Burke's book is one among several recent attempts to consider the eunuch alongside gender and sexuality.[4] And Eric Barreto's work on ethnicity in Acts reminds us that although ethnic differences worked differently in the ancient world, they nevertheless were important ways for people to understand themselves and each other and powerful tools for ancient empires to exploit![5]

---

[1] Clarice J. Martin, "A Chamberlain's Journey and the Challenge of Interpretation for Liberation," *Semeia* 47 (1989): 105–35.

[2] Zorodzai Dube, "The Ethiopian Eunuch in Transit: A Migrant Theoretical Perspective," *HTS Teologiese Studies/Theological Studies* 69, no. 1 (2019).

[3] Manuel Villalobos, "Bodies del Otro Lado: Finding Life and Hope in the Borderland: Gloria Anzaldúa, the Ethiopian Eunuch of Acts 8:26–40, y Yo," in *Bible Trouble: Queer Reading at the Boundaries of Biblical Scholarship*, ed. Teresa J. Hornsby and Ken Stone, Semeia Studies 67 (SBL, 2011).

[4] Sean D. Burke, *Queering the Ethiopian Eunuch: Strategies of Ambiguity in Acts*, Emerging Scholars (Fortress Press, 2013).

[5] Eric D. Barreto, *Ethnic Negotiations: The Function of Race and Ethnicity in Acts 16* (Mohr Siebeck, 2010).

4

Voices on the Edges

A few years ago I was passing through a town where some old friends lived, and we made arrangements to grab lunch together on a Sunday. As I get older, I value those kinds of gatherings more and more because—despite the ways social media can keep us connected—it is easy to lose touch with people as the years go by. We spent about an hour and a half catching up on each other's careers, families, and emerging middle-age hobbies and ailments.

Then, as we were close to finishing our time together, one of my friends suddenly got cagey. "Oh my God, my pastor is here," he said, glancing over at the other side of the restaurant, where a family was being shown to their booth. "I missed church to meet up with you, but if he sees me here he will realize that I skipped church to eat lunch in a restaurant." In the moment, I thought it was kind of funny. As a minister myself, I always like to see people in church, but I would never judge anyone for *not* coming to church, either; I don't have any expectation that church should be a person's all-consuming obsession. But in the small town where he lived, my friend felt as if he lived in a fishbowl, his actions constantly open to his pastor's and other religious folks' scrutiny, and that meeting an old friend for lunch instead of going to church would be just the kind of thing of which they would disapprove. And as the after-church crowd filled the restaurant, I could sense other diners making the same calculation, and a faint tension seemed to run between the church-skippers and the church-goers.

I grew up in a small town where most everyone went to church. But my family didn't—at least not when I was in elementary school. We lived across the street from one of the town's biggest Baptist churches, an imposing and soaring brick structure, and we were two doors down from a quaint Episcopal church with white wood siding. On Sunday mornings our normally quiet street was busy with cars coming and going for church services and families dressed in their Sunday best walking with their Bibles from the parking lots to the pews. My parents always asked my brother and me to stay inside on Sunday mornings—not to play in the front yard or ride our bikes up and down the street—because they didn't want all the church folks to notice that we weren't sitting in the pews. Everyone *knew* we weren't in church, of course. But there was something about being *seen* not going to church that felt culturally dangerous. As my friend tried in vain to hide from his pastor's view in that restaurant, I thought about those Sunday mornings stuck in our house.

Every time a survey of religious participation in the United States is released, the numbers are down. People identify less and less with religion in the United States, and the numbers are the worst for Protestant mainline Christianity, the branch of Christianity to which I belong. Even when people say they are Christian, they are less likely than before to say they belong to any particular religious community. In Denver, where I live, the latest Pew Research Center Religious Landscape Study says that about 53 percent of the population identifies as Christian and 39 percent is religiously unaffiliated. Only 18 percent of the population reports attending a religious service (of any kind) weekly or more frequently.[1] In the South, where my friend lives, the numbers for participation and identification are higher. But even there, participation has been declining for years; and there, too, the numbers of people who say they identify with any particular religious tradition at all have been falling. My friend's sense of obligation to attend church—and his sense of panic at the possibility of being found out for *not* attending—might soon be a thing of the past.

My friend and I both grew up in a world where religion was very important, a world where church attendance and participation were social norms. But that world is increasingly disappearing as religious affiliation recedes in the United States and participation in mainline Protestant Christianity in particular collapses. In Denver, among people my age, I am one of the only people I know who go to church at all, and it's almost unheard of among people younger than me. The numbers bear out a stark generational divide. That Pew Research study found that while about 80 percent of adults age seventy-four years and older identify as Christian, among adults age eighteen to twenty-four that number is only 46 percent.

Anecdotally, the people around my age and younger with whom I talk report many reasons for not going to church. One major reason is belief: people simply don't believe the theological claims that churches make. Another reason is time. People cherish their weekends and often need to use that Sunday morning time for kids' sporting events, projects at home, or rest.

Perhaps the most common thing I hear is that Christianity's close association with right-wing American politics has pushed people away from

---

[1] "People in the Denver Metro Area," Religious Landscape Study, Pew Research Center, 2023, https://www.pewresearch.org/religious-landscape-study/metro-area/denver-co/.

church. Beginning in the 1980s and continuing to the present day, the so-called "religious right" has exerted a strong influence on American politics, polarizing the country around issues like abortion, LGBTQIA+ rights, and religion in public schools. While these actions by the religious right have energized many Americans (leading to gains in evangelical churches and victories for conservative politicians), they have turned many people off religion altogether. Many people tell me they don't want to be associated with what Christianity has been doing in America.

We therefore find ourselves in a moment when some forms of Christianity are tightly associated with certain political parties, policies, and politicians, while other forms of Christianity—including the mainline Protestantism of which I am a part—are on the outside looking in. As more conservative Christians claim space at the center of American public life, progressive Christians feel pushed to the margins. That experience of marginality—the sense of being on the outside of something looking in—is new to the Protestant mainline (especially the *White* Protestant mainline), which for most of its existence has lived at the center of American cultural and religious life. Now, in the second Trump Administration, in another moment of triumph for politicians who are closely associated with the religious right, we on the religious left find ourselves in the wilderness. How can we speak from the margins?

How Does Marginality Work?

There are many forms of marginality and many ways people can find themselves on the margins of something. Sometimes marginality is cultural, racial or ethnic, or related to gender or sexuality. Other times it's economic or political, or it comes from some other experience of being at odds with dominant systems. In this chapter, I'm most interested in the newfound marginality of Protestant mainline Christianity, in the current political climate, as it relates to the Book of Acts. But the ways of thinking found in this chapter might be useful for considering other kinds of marginality, too. And it will be my argument, at the end of the chapter, that the experience of feeling marginal to the political culture of the United States might be just what the Protestant mainline needs to begin paying real and close attention to some of those other kinds of marginality.

In the last chapter about territory, I used the metaphor of center and periphery. Every empire has a center, and it spreads outward from there, acquiring ("eating") territory. And—as I argued in the last chapter—empires tend to work by ransacking those peripheral territories for resources and protection and drawing money and goods and safety back toward the center. In the Roman Empire, the capital of Rome and the people there at the center grew wealthy, while the places and people at the peripheries got squeezed.

But empires are about more than money, and other kinds of systems—like culture and religion—also have centers and peripheries. In *this* chapter, I am less interested in physical territory and more interested in the way people find themselves in positions of lesser or greater connection, esteem, or honor. In the previous section, I talked about how certain forms of American Christianity have declined in popularity and prestige. The Book of Acts is interested in these same kinds of questions. Several of Acts' stories turn on the dynamics of marginality, with some of its heroes consistently portrayed as being on the outside of respectability or power. Acts tells the story of the Jesus Movement's beginnings and its first ventures into the Roman world, but it tells that story decidedly from the margins.

How does marginality work? Every social system has insiders and outsiders. We have all experienced this at work, in families, in friend groups, or—to cite the most iconic example—at the school lunch table. We have probably all felt like an insider to something, and we all probably also know what it feels like to be an outsider. Human beings are social creatures, and we have subtle but powerful ways to signal to each other who belongs and who does not. Historically, churches have made many people feel as if they were on the outside. American Christianity usually has been profoundly racially segregated, for example, and people whose gender or sexuality or class doesn't fit the norms often have felt excluded and pushed out. That's a big part of the reason the church now finds itself on the outside of American culture looking in—because the church often has been the place where those kinds of marginality have played out, and many folks have shunned churches because they rightly associate church with exclusion.

Let's think about social centrality and marginality from two perspectives—first from the perspective of the people at the center, then from the perspective of the people on the margins.

From the center, social systems feel good. It feels good to belong to something—to feel as if you have an important place among your people. At the center of a powerful system, you probably aren't thinking of yourself as an agent of exclusion. Instead, you're probably thinking of yourself as someone who belongs to a group of like-minded people—birds of a feather who flock together. I have noticed this dynamic myself at the two churches where I have served in my career. Both churches had a strong sense of internal identity and coherence. Both churches knew just what kind of people they were for, theologically speaking, and both were intentional about making space for people who had been excluded from those spaces in the past. Both churches, therefore, thought of themselves as very welcoming. And they *were* welcoming—if you were the kind of person those churches imagined themselves to be serving. If asked whether they were concerned about people on the margins of their communities, both churches would have answered *yes*, emphatically, and they would have meant it.

But in both cases, the churches where I have worked have been White, middle-class institutions. In both cases, the people who showed up at the building usually wore nice clothing, drove nice cars, and had nice jobs. The worship style of both churches was relatively reserved, in the White mainline Protestant tradition, and the clergy at both places (including me) were very well educated. Even though both churches made a big deal about wanting to welcome everyone, neither was especially successful at it because all the ways they had of being themselves—their worship style, their race and class, their style and aesthetics—felt exclusionary to others, even if that exclusion was unintended. Some of the people who showed up at those churches felt welcome—like they belonged. But others felt excluded and pushed to the margins. No matter how much those churches *said* that they were welcoming of people who didn't already feel as if they belonged, the churches were still sending signals, albeit unintentional signals, that made people feel marginalized.

I'm using the example of churches here for several reasons. This is a book about the Bible, after all, and it's a chapter focusing on churches. But I'm also using the example of churches because churches (at least Protestant mainline churches, and especially White ones) have experienced a dramatic flip from the center to the margins. Whereas once White mainline Protestantism was one of the most stable institutions in American life and enjoyed incredible proximity to power, now it finds itself on the outside. My friend felt the old power of Christianity at our restaurant lunch that Sunday; he felt how Christianity could compel him to act in certain ways, just as my parents did when they asked me to play inside on Sundays so it wouldn't be obvious that we were missing church. But that old power is waning quickly, and church is increasingly marginal to American society. So what now?

Marginality in the Book of Acts

The Acts of the Apostles tells a heroes' tale, but it tells that tale with a surprising amount of marginality. The characters of Acts—people like Paul, the other apostles, and the Ethiopian eunuch—are consistently shown to be on the outside of power structures, relegated to the margins. For a book that's so aware of power structures such as empire, autocracy, and religious establishments, Acts works overtime to make sure its readers know its most important characters were *not* very important.

I'll start with my favorite example of this because it shows just the opposite of what most people think. In Acts 17:16–34, Paul visits Athens—the intellectual capital of the ancient Mediterranean world and the past home of many famous philosophers like Socrates, Aristotle, and Plato. The first time I became aware of this story from Acts, I was a student at Mars Hill College (which is now Mars Hill University), and I was in the college bookstore shopping for T-shirts. I had a vague memory from the campus tour that the school was named for something about the Bible, but looking at a particular shirt in the bookstore, I noticed Acts 17:22 (in the King James Version) printed on it: "Then Paul stood in the midst of Mars' Hill, and said, 'Ye men of Athens, I perceive that in all things ye are too superstitious.'"

That caught my attention! I did a little asking around, and I learned that the college had been founded with the name Mars Hill because that was the name of the place where Paul, in Acts, had brought the best of religious proclamation into conversation with the best of intellectual work. Mars' Hill (often left untranslated as the *Areopagus* in many Bible translations and on the tours of the spot in Athens) was the place where Paul brought the message of Jesus to the ancient community of intellectual inquiry that was centered in Athens. It was sort of like bringing a revival to Harvard, I was told, or preaching a sermon to the physics department at Oxford—a glorious moment of contact between the religious world and the academic world. What better metaphor for an institution founded by religious folks to educate young people?

I bought the T-shirt (long since worn out and grown too small and discarded), and because of that experience I have stayed interested in Acts 17. When I became a Bible scholar, I began thinking more deeply about it, and—reading the passage alongside postcolonial theory—I began to notice the ways the story of triumph didn't quite add up. Postcolonial theory is a branch of critical theory that pays attention to how power works in colonial systems—in political systems of domination and resource extraction, not so different from the systems I described in the last chapter. With the help of those theorists, I began to notice that Paul's trip to Athens was less of a triumph and more of an ordeal—an experience of marginalization that Paul simply had to endure. Usually Christians tell the story as Paul's brave, confident, and successful foray into Athens' cutthroat intellectualism. Acts tells it quite differently. It says Paul never *intended* to go to Athens or to preach there, that others "left" him there (17:15), and that he "was waiting for them" there (17:16) without much to do. Moreover, Paul didn't *decide* to give his triumphant sermon on Mars' Hill. Instead, the people who looked down on him sort of bullied him into giving that sermon. "Also some Epicurean and Stoic philosophers debated with him," Acts 17:18 tells us, naming some of the dominant philosophical schools of the time. "Some said, 'What does this pretentious babbler want to say?' Others said, 'He seems to be a proclaimer of foreign divinities.'" The word "babbler" in 17:18 is a curious word in Greek. It means, literally, "seed-picker," and while scholars aren't in total agreement about what it means, they do agree that it was *not* a compliment. Paul once again stepped up not because he wanted to but because someone else forced him. "So they took him and brought him to the Areopagus and asked him" to explain himself. "It sounds rather strange to us, so we would like to know what it means" (17:19–20). Yikes.

That's where that verse from the T-shirt came in, and that's where Paul gave his sermon. The speech itself is quite elegant, at least as Luke records it. It is a meditation on the ways unknown things had been revealed in the God of Israel and the ways the God of Israel was the one for whom the Athenians had been searching for all along.

Paul was doing his best, but tellingly, he didn't quote Jesus or anything from Hebrew scripture. Instead, Paul quoted a Greek philosopher and a poet—the kind of people Paul reckoned the Athenians would recognize and respect. Paul was trying, desperately, to make himself understood and understandable to the intellectuals in Athens, going so far as to parrot back to them the sources of wisdom he thought they would admire. But in the end, after his sermon, Acts tells us that "some scoffed; but others said, 'We will hear you again about this,'" (17:32) and a few became believers. It could have gone worse, but it was hardly a triumph.

Christian tradition *treats* this story like a triumph, but I think that's a mistake. I don't think Acts intended Paul's visit to Athens to look like a triumph. Instead, I think that Acts intended it to show how marginal Paul and the Jesus Movement were to the broader world. The episode in Athens certainly could have been an opportunity for Luke to portray Paul as an equal to the Athenian elite, holding his own and mixing it up among the heirs of Plato and Aristotle. But that's not what Luke did. Instead, Luke showed how the elite had disdain for Paul and for his message—how they rejected him as a "seed-picker" who failed to impress. Luke told the story of Paul in Athens just as he might tell the story of an awkward kid at the middle school lunch table: as someone brought along just to be ridiculed by the cooler kids.

That pattern shows up elsewhere in Acts. Even when the apostles did impressive things, the people around them usually didn't credit them with it. Think of the passage in Acts 2—the story of Pentecost. That story tells about the apostles' remarkable and sudden linguistic ability. It's a story about how the apostles suddenly were able to speak in a variety of foreign languages that they had not previously spoken. But the reaction of the crowd was to scoff at them, notice that they were Galileans (not, apparently, a group of people usually known for linguistic diversity or academic achievements), and wonder out loud whether they were all drunk. Or think of the several scenes of apostles running afoul of the Jerusalem establishment in Acts 4 (Peter and John brought before the Jerusalem council), Acts 7 (Stephen's speech to the council), and Acts 21–26 (Paul's arrest in the temple in Jerusalem and subsequent trials and appearances before rulers). In all those cases, the apostles were met with skepticism and were treated as outsiders who had reached beyond their station. In each of those stories people responded to the apostles with an attitude of *Who do these people think that they are?*

One of Acts' great marginal figures—literally marginal, in some senses—is the Ethiopian eunuch, whom we met in the previous chapter. Acts almost goes out of its way to show how marginal the eunuch is. In conceptions of ancient geography, Ethiopia was literally on the margins, or beyond them—too far to the south to be reckoned in many Roman understandings of the known world. The eunuch was, well, a eunuch, and in those days that represented an identity that didn't fit with the way most people understood or accepted gender. Luke even set the eunuch's story in a marginal place—a nowhere-place abstracted from landmarks and familiar spaces, a "wilderness road" to which Philip had to be directed and from which Philip had to be whisked, almost teleported, by the Spirit of the Lord once their encounter was over. Luke could hardly have written about the Ethiopian eunuch more marginally than he did. Yet the eunuch represents a critical part of Acts' narrative of bearing witness "to the ends of the earth," which in itself is a marginal idea.

That's a pattern in Acts: its heroes are often from or in the margins, and its villains are often the people at the center of power. Think back to the story of the enslaved girl from whom Paul cast a spirit of divination in Acts 16. This girl's "spirit of the Python" tied her closely to the cultic site of Delphi and its famous temples and oracle. Paul doesn't exactly come across as heroic in that story (more like petty), and the enslaved girl doesn't come across as a villain. But the girl's owners were certainly villainous, and the way the story develops into a full-blown crisis once Paul cast out the spirit, landing Paul and Silas in prison, certainly made Paul into a hero. This is a story, then, in which representatives of Jesus (Paul and Silas) clashed with representatives of one of the ancient world's most venerable and famous cultic sites (the enslaved girl, but really her owners) and came out on top. Again and again, Acts makes sure the reader knows that while the power lay at the center of important traditions, social groups, and institutions, the Jesus Movement operated squarely outside of those centers of power and that just like Jesus himself, the heroes of the faith always came from the margins.

Living in the Margins

For a long time, it has been ironic that the stories of Christianity's origins came from the margins because Christianity itself has been so central to the story of worldly power, including in the United States. Christianity has wielded prestige and accumulated uncountable wealth, and it has thrown its weight around in a way that pushed many people to the margins. Christian theology backed conquerors and emperors, and it justified wars and conquest and slaughter. Christian doctrine imposed moral standards that left many people shunned and discarded by their communities and their families. Christians argued in favor of slavery, Christians fought for segregation, and Christians made Jim Crow a central part of American culture.

Yet that central place of power in the world is at odds with the ways the New Testament describes Christianity's origins. Acts tells the story of the Jesus Movement as the story of marginal people running afoul of the law. And somehow Christianity took those stories and turned itself into the power behind the law itself.

Now, faced with diminishing social, cultural, economic, and political power, Christianity finds itself on the outside again—at least certain forms of Christianity do, in the United States. We who call ourselves Christians should think of this as a gift. Christianity, in my opinion, was never meant to occupy the center. Christianity can never follow its calling when it holds positions of power. So Protestant mainline Christianity's current position on the margins of American society might be just the thing we need to be the people God calls us to be. Jesus lived on the margins and died there too. The apostles, as Acts reminds us repeatedly, moved on the margins of their world, and they constantly took on the institutions and the people at the center of power. It's an ancient pattern that we now find ourselves repeating.

Those of us who now live in the United States—those of us who have lived to see the simultaneous decline of the church and the rise of autocracy—have an opportunity. Although it never feels good to be on the outside of things looking in, that's actually a powerful position to occupy. For like many of the first figures of the early Christian tradition—the ones whom the New Testament treats like heroes—were similarly marginal to their world. Like them, occupying the margins today affords us an opportunity to speak into the center and to call out the people with power and hold them accountable in a way that we could not do if we ourselves were powerful or central. In this moment our nation needs prophetic and critical moral voices, for many of the leading political, cultural, and even religious voices are advocating cruelty, greed, and violence. Perhaps God has put us back at the margins for just such a time as this, to speak with conviction and purpose and to stand up for all the others who live at the margins too—for immigrants, for racial and ethnic and religious minorities, for people of diverse genders and sexualities, for women who are once more being pushed aside, and for poor people who always seem to be forgotten. Finding ourselves on the margins, perhaps we, like the apostles in Acts, will realize we are exactly where we need to be.

Further Reading

This chapter deals a lot with the changing landscape of American religion and especially with the changing place of White Protestant mainline Christianity in the story of American Christianity. One way to convey this is telling the story of the rise of White Evangelicalism, which has largely displaced mainline Protestantism in positions of power. Among the influential recent books on that subject is *Jesus and John Wayne* by Kristin Kobes Du Mez.[2] Another is Tony Keddie's book *Republican Jesus*.[3]

In this chapter I mentioned postcolonial theory. If you are interested in learning more about how postcolonial theory works and how to use it to read and interpret the Bible, R.S. Sugirtharajah's writings are a great place to start. The book *The Postcolonial Bible,* which he edited, is a classic,[4] and a more recent one is *Exploring Postcolonial Biblical Criticism*.[5] For another take on the question of "the margins" and biblical interpretation, my colleague Miguel De La Torre's book *The Politics of Jesús* is a great starting point.[6]

If you are interested in a fuller version of my argument about Paul in Athens, you'll find it in my book *To the Ends of the Earth: The Necropolitics of the Acts of the Apostles*.[7] And I'll once again suggest *The Story Luke Tells* by Justo González as a good book that frames both Luke and Acts as stories told from and to the margins, with an emphasis on the power of marginality to disrupt the center and the powerful structures of the world.[8]

---

[2] Kristin Kobes Du Mez, *Jesus and John Wayne: How White Evangelicals Corrupted a Faith and Fractured a Nation* (Liveright, 2020).

[3] Tony Keddie, *Republican Jesus* (University of California Press, 2020).

[4] R.S. Sugirtharajah, ed., *The Postcolonial Bible* (Sheffield Academic Press, 1998).

[5] R.S. Sugirtharajah, *Exploring Postcolonial Biblical Criticism: History, Method, Practice* (Wiley-Blackwell, 2012).

[6] Miguel De La Torre, *The Politics of Jesús: A Hispanic Political Theology* (Rowman & Littlefield, 2015).

[7] Eric C. Smith, *To the Ends of the Earth: The Necropolitics of the Acts of the Apostles* (SBL, 2026).

[8] Justo L. González, *The Story Luke Tells: Luke's Unique Witness to the Gospel* (William B. Eerdmans, 2015).

PART II

The Strategies of Autocracy and Empire

Part II of this book focuses on how autocrats use their power. It considers how empires and autocracies gain and maintain control over people and how systems maintain and enhance the power of leaders. Here you'll find chapters on unjust criminal justice systems (which carry out justice differently for different kinds of people), incarceration (which is often used as a tool of control), violence (used to cow the population and make people afraid of resisting), and the protection of money rather than people (a hallmark of systems in which the objective is not good governance but the enrichment of the leaders). By pointing out such patterns of authoritarian states and empires, these chapters help us to recognize how those patterns are at work in the Book of Acts and in our world today.

5

Unjust Criminal Justice Systems

A quarter-century ago, when I was a divinity school student, I needed some extra course credits in my final semester before earning my degree. I scanned the schedule and chose a night class based solely on its title: "The Theology and Politics of Crime and Justice in America." I had little prior experience thinking about criminal justice, much less studying it academically, but the course title grabbed my attention, and I signed up.

Harmon Wray taught the course on Thursday nights, and I quickly grew to admire him for his quiet but fiery commitment to justice. Wray was a longtime activist and academic in Nashville. Years before that he had written most of a doctoral dissertation before deciding his efforts were better spent on more practical matters, and he devoted his life to advocacy and interventionist work in Tennessee's criminal justice system. At the time I was enrolled in his class, Wray was focused mostly on his work with the Tennessee Coalition to Abolish State Killing, a group fighting the death penalty in Tennessee, and working on behalf of death row inmates. He also worked with a number of other groups, like the Restorative Justice Coalition of Tennessee, the Tennessee Hunger Coalition, and Tennesseans for Handgun Control. I remember these because our class meetings often were punctuated by Wray's strident updates about the work of those groups—a vigil organized ahead of someone's appeal hearing, a petition being circulated, the news from the legislative session at the state capitol. It was eye-opening for me to be in the presence of someone so utterly devoted to justice work and so completely consumed by it, and to see up close the way the very idea of "criminal justice" evaporated under theological scrutiny.

That was my biggest takeaway from the course—that "criminal justice" as an idea and as an American practice was both theologically grounded and theologically bankrupt. We spent a lot of time in the course thinking about the so-called "prison-industrial complex" (more on that in the next chapter), but we also spent time noticing how the criminal justice systems that put people *into* the prison-industrial complex were broken, biased, and ineffective at doing the things they claimed to do. We noticed that when you look at the rationales for our systems of prosecution and punishment, and when you look at the ways those systems are sold to the public, Christian theology often sat just beneath the surface. Our society had ransacked Christian theology to build ideas like criminality and restitution, so crime has come to look like sin and courts and prison like purgatory and hell—in short, like absolutely righteous punishment for people who were allegedly categorically evil.

But while criminal justice systems used the language of theology—words like redemption, guilt, reconciliation, and penance—those same systems actually ran on money. What was being sold as theology, or justice, was actually capitalism. Prisons were, at that time, rapidly privatizing, so a whole new set of market forces was pushing people into the criminal justice system and incentivizing incarceration. When prisons are private and for-profit institutions, locked-up human bodies become the product.

We also talked a lot about race in that class, beginning with the ways capitalism was not new to the criminal justice system, but noting that some of the earliest mega-prisons in the United States were created after the Civil War to ensure a steady supply of free labor to replace the workforce of emancipated formerly enslaved people in the South. We thought about the stark racial disparities in criminal justice systems—the ways people of color (and especially Black people) are much, much more likely to be arrested, charged, tried, convicted, and imprisoned than White people are, and the ways those disparities have their roots in America's history of racist violence and the commodification of Black bodies.

I learned a great deal in that course that reframed how I thought about the relationships between criminal justice, theology, and race. But it wasn't until a decade or so later that I read a book that completely transformed my understanding of how race not only *influenced* criminal justice in America but actually *determined* it.

That book was Michelle Alexander's 2012 *The New Jim Crow: Mass Incarceration in the Age of Colorblindness.*[1] It was a huge bestseller, and the book brought the conversation about America's relationship with criminal justice into the mainstream. Having taken Harmon Wray's class in divinity school, I wasn't really surprised by Alexander's thesis and argument that the American criminal justice system is racially biased. What was astonishing about the book, and what remains remarkable even after all these years have passed since its

[1] Michelle Alexander, *The New Jim Crow: Mass Incarceration in the Age of Colorblindness* (The New Press, 2012).

publication, is the way Alexander collected mountains of evidence to back up and flesh out those claims. Alexander's book is dense and long. Story after story tells of how the whole system—from policing to the courts to jails and prisons—reinforces and perpetuates racial bias.

After reading Alexander's book, it's difficult to hold the view that racism has merely influenced or tainted the criminal justice system. Instead, the reader understands quite clearly that racism *is* the criminal justice system—that the system exists, from top to bottom, as a way to enforce racial hierarchies and to ensure that America's racist caste system remains intact.

Perhaps that sounds extreme if you haven't read the book, but Alexander makes an airtight case, and I encourage you to read it for yourself. Alexander would no doubt acknowledge that the *people* who work in those systems—she is herself an attorney and legal scholar—do not necessarily hold racist views or work to uphold racist hierarchies. Instead, she points to the ways the *systems* themselves function, independent of what the individuals involved in them might desire or do, and the ways the *systems* collect and aggregate America's histories and biases into one place. If anything, Alexander's research has become only more relevant in the years since her book was published, and the patterns she describes—including racially motivated policing, prosecution, and incarceration—have only continued to intensify.

This dynamic between individuals and systems is important to remember as we think about criminal justice and its place in society, then as we think about how criminal justice systems work in the Book of Acts. Although Acts describes various encounters between the apostles and individual representatives of the Roman justice system, Acts' descriptions of those encounters always have more to do with the (absurd, futile, and theologically bankrupt) systems those individuals represent than with the particular individual representative of Roman power who happens to be in the courtroom. The Book of Acts describes a Roman justice system that systematically disregarded the very thing it was supposed to cherish—justice—and that treated human beings carelessly and with casual cruelty.

In that regard, Roman justice in the Book of Acts is not so different from the justice systems we encounter in the United States today: ineffective, unconcerned with the roles of bias and unfairness in the process, and driven by ideas and concerns that don't always have much to do with the truth of any given situation.

These conditions have only intensified in the United States since Alexander's book was published. As I write this book, the United States' immigration court system is being gutted by the firings of longtime judges and the extrajudicial detentions and deportations of millions of people. Current U.S. policy now makes official for brown-skinned people what Alexander showed has long been happening under the surface for black-skinned people: having non-white skin is often reason enough for someone to scoop you up, put you in jail, prosecute you, and take away your liberty, whether you are guilty of anything or not. If you have been paying close attention to our criminal justice and immigration systems for a while, that might not surprise you. What *might* surprise you is how much the Book of Acts has to say about it.

How Does Criminal Justice Work?

If you visit the homepage of the United States Department of Justice, you'll find the department's mission statement. "The mission of the Department of Justice is to uphold the rule of law," it says, "to keep our country safe, and to protect civil rights." That's a pretty good summary of how most of us think about justice. Justice is about the "rule of law," the security and safety that come from the law, and the equal protection the law is supposed to afford each of us as we live our lives. Systems of justice are supposed to act as guarantors of that security, safety, and equal protection.

As long as there have been societies with laws, there have been systems for sorting through the interpretations of those laws and how they apply to specific cases. Those systems have varied widely over the years. Sometimes the system has been simply that more powerful people get to do what they want and less powerful people can't do much about it. Sometimes a king or a queen has been the judge of which laws applied and when, and whatever they said became true (or at least was enforced). And sometimes societies have created whole infrastructures for creating, enforcing, and adjudicating laws.

The idea that justice and the law ought to be impartial has popped up a few times in history, in several different societies, and in different times and places. But the notion of legal impartiality that we hold in the United States—what we sometimes call "the rule of law"—is a relatively recent idea. We mostly inherited this idea from Europe in the period of the Enlightenment, and especially from England, where people were beginning to question just how much absolute power kings should have. As we in the United States constrained the power of monarchs and increased the power of the people (at least the power of *some* of the people), the idea of "the rule of law" emerged as a way to say that everyone (or at least *some* everyones) ought to receive equal and fair treatment in the eyes of the law. Justice began to consist of figuring out what the law required, determining how the law had been followed or broken in a given situation, and meting out punishments accordingly.

That ideal has played out differently for different people. Class, wealth, status, gender, race, and social connections always to some extent have determined how justice systems treat people. That's true in the modern world, as scholars like Michelle Alexander have shown, and it was true in the ancient world too. The Book of Acts seems especially interested in putting its readers inside the Roman criminal justice system, and it returns to those settings again and again. So let's look at some of the scenes from various moments in Acts when someone—often Paul—is faced with a moment of legal judgment.

Criminal Justice in Acts

Again and again, Luke takes the reader of Acts into legal scenes. One almost begins to wonder whether Luke had some special interest in the field of law or otherwise somehow found himself watching court proceedings as a kind of hobby. Most likely Luke knew that Acts' many courtroom scenes had happened but he was not actually present there himself for most of the scenes he describes. Perhaps Luke gained information about the apostles' encounters with the Roman justice system from eyewitnesses, or perhaps he pieced scenes together from things he had heard or read. In any event, Luke shows a steady attention to such moments.

The first of these scenes comes early in Acts, in 4:1–22, and it foreshadows something important about the way justice systems work: justice in Acts is always a little situational, somewhat informal, and very driven by the powers of persuasion of the people involved. Just prior to this, as described at the end of Acts 3, John and Peter had been preaching in the Jerusalem temple and drawing a crowd, and this had brought them to the attention of the priesthood in charge of the temple precincts. The temple captain (who would have worked under the chief priest and would have been charged with handling just such situations in which someone was creating a scene or disturbance in the temple) arrested John and Peter. The temple captain had the two of them brought into custody, and the next day a group of powerful people—"their rulers, elders, and scribes … with Annas, the high priest, Caiaphas, John, and Alexander, and all who were of the high-priestly family" (4:5–6) —gathered to consider their case. (It's worth pointing out that Annas was the high priest from the years 6 to 15, long before this story took place, so Luke has either mistakenly included him here or has added him because of Annas' fame as a way to raise the stakes of the gathering and make Peter and John seem important).

This was not a Roman trial by any means: it was a council constituted of leaders within the Jewish religious establishment and the officials connected to the temple. But it *was* a body that had an intense interest in the question of authority and in the ways in which people's behavior transgressed the boundaries of proper conduct. "By what power or by what name did you do this?" (4:7) asked the assembled men. They wanted to know why the apostles, who were not priests or temple officials, had felt empowered to preach so publicly in the temple. Peter responded to the men's question with an eloquent and theologically rich speech. And "when they saw the boldness of Peter and John and realized that they were uneducated and ordinary men" (4:13), the council first deliberated then asked the two men to cease their behavior. Defiantly, John and Peter promptly declared they would not follow the order. Somehow despite that, they were let go.

This is an early legal confrontation in Acts—a small-scale and low-stakes version of some of the conflicts that explode later in the book. But already we can see the importance of power and authority, and already Acts is focusing on questions of the relationship between the early Jesus Movement and the world into which it was emerging. "By what power or by what name did you do this?" is a perfectly reasonable question for a system of justice to ask, and the apostles' answer—essentially, that God had authorized them—was honestly a difficult one for the council to evaluate or adjudicate.

More examples of legal confrontations follow. We have already looked at the case of Stephen, who (in chapters 6 and 7) came before a similar council—not a Roman legal body but a local Jerusalem-based religious and political council charged with maintaining order and decorum. Following Stephen's case, we can skip ahead to chapter 16, where Acts tells about a series of confrontations between mobs, local authorities, and Paul and his companions that stretches all the way to chapter 19. In the cities of Philippi, Thessalonica, and Ephesus, in chapters 16, 17, and 19 respectively, the apostles came to the attention of the authorities because of some kind of public mob action.

In chapter 16, we find Paul and Silas in Philippi, which we have already seen in an earlier chapter. When her owners became angry after Paul cast out of the enslaved girl the spirit of divination, "they seized Paul and Silas and dragged them into the marketplace before the authorities" (16:19) and brought them to the "magistrates." Here, Luke gives us a very transparent and accurate view into Roman governance. Legal proceedings did indeed often take place in the marketplace, which was an open communal public space. And Roman colonies like Philippi were in fact governed by magistrates, who served as Rome's representatives in local affairs.

Luke portrays a chaotic scene in Philippi. After the owners of the enslaved girl brought Paul and Silas to the magistrates in the marketplace, Acts tells us, the crowd began to attack them—though it's not clear whether those attacks were verbal or physical. Then the magistrates had Paul and Silas stripped, severely flogged, and thrown into prison. Today, this is barely recognizable to us as a legal scene. There were no police involved, there were no charges, and there was certainly no presumption of innocence (which is a modern idea). The magistrates seemed to be uninterested in finding out any information from Paul and Silas about what they might have done, and neither did they seem to spend much time testing the claims of the girl's owners. The way Luke tells the story, it was a mob scene designed to humiliate and injure Paul and Silas. That might, in fact, be what was going on. The magistrates might have been beating Paul and Silas on the presumption that they were guilty, or to teach them a lesson, or to make an example of them for others. Or they might have stripped and beaten and imprisoned them because Paul and Silas were not forthcoming with information and they wanted to make them confess to something.

This story of Paul and Silas in Philippi is well known not because of this "trial" scene but because of the midnight jailbreak that came afterward. Beginning in Acts 16:25, as Paul and Silas were sitting in jail, we learn about an earthquake that opened the prison doors and broke apart everyone's chains. This was a catastrophe for the jailer who, on realizing that his prisoners have escaped, prepared to kill himself in shame. But Paul stopped him and, to make a long story short, the two apostles ended up breakfasting with the jailer's family and baptizing the whole lot of them. It's a very tidy ending to what began as a very messy story. As an added bonus, the magistrates sent the police to let Paul and Silas go, but the apostles refused to hear it from the police. They wanted an apology from the magistrates themselves, and the two of them sent word back to that effect, including one powerful detail: that Paul and Silas were Romans. Suddenly the magistrates themselves were there apologizing, saying it was all a big misunderstanding and sending Paul and Silas on their way.

This is a wild story, but there are some important things to notice about it. First, notice the role of shame and violence in the justice system. The first action of the magistrates, before ascertaining charges or hearing any evidence, was to strip and beat their prisoners. That haste came back to bite them when they later learned that they had stripped and beaten Roman citizens. But their first instinct, as representatives of Roman justice, was violence. Notice also how much of a difference it makes when Paul announces that they are citizens and not simply common subjects. The Roman justice system provided starkly different outcomes to different kinds of people. Slaves could be treated harshly, and common folks could be beaten and tortured and punished without many restrictions. But citizens held a range of protections and privileges that other people could not access.

This might seem like an absurd way to pursue justice—beat first, ask questions later—but it is not all that different from our own system. Different people receive wildly different outcomes from our justice system depending on their ability to pay attorneys, their skin color, and (especially recently) their suspected or actual immigration status. As the work of scholars like Michelle Alexander demonstrates, our own systems are not much better than Philippi's. We too see some people slide right out of the criminal justice system (like Paul and Silas did once they announced their citizenship) while others get ensnared in it long term. And just like in Philippi, much of the violence of our system happens right up front, before people have even been charged, much less tried and convicted. The Trump Administration's immigration crackdown has led to many people being imprisoned in newly built ICE facilities without access to proper legal proceedings, and many of those facilities are reported to have horrible conditions.[2] In some cases—most famously the case of Kilmar Abrego Garcia, but in many other cases too—people are being deported to *other* countries' prisons, where conditions can be even less humane and sometimes meet the legal definitions of torture.[3] These imprisonments and deportations are happening before people gain access to legal representation and before their cases can be adjudicated by courts.

After Paul and Silas were released from the Philippian prison, they quickly found themselves in hot water again, this time in nearby Thessalonica. But it wasn't Paul and Silas themselves who landed in trouble in Thessalonica, but a man named Jason, whom we talked about briefly in chapter 2. After a mob couldn't find Paul and Silas, they settled on Jason ("and some brothers and sisters") and brought them to the city authorities. In the case of Jason and his companions, the city officials charged them bail and released them. That was good news for Jason and his friends, but they probably left the experience wondering how they had ended up being dragged in front of the city officials. From their perspective (and perhaps from our perspective too) the workings of the Thessalonian justice system seemed fairly arbitrary and capricious.

The final act in this series of mob-induced legal scenes is the most serious of the three in terms of the threat it posed to Paul and his companions. The incident happened in Ephesus, and already in chapter 2 we spent some time looking at the story. In some ways this episode is similar to the one in Philippi,

---

[2] Christine Fernando, "Judge hears testimony about crowded cells and overflowing toilets at Chicago-area immigration site," Associated Press, November 4, 2025, https://apnews.com/article/chicago-illinois-immigration-ice-broadview-c1cce6344d39da317179f3619daa026a.

[3] Scott Neuman, "Abrego Garcia Says He Was Severely Beaten in Salvadoran Prison," NPR, July 3, 2025, https://www.npr.org/2025/07/03/g-s1-75775/abrego-garcia-el-salvador-prison-beaten-torture.

since in both cases the local folks were worried that Paul's preaching was going to put a dent in their finances, and in both cases those financial concerns (which we will consider more fully in chapter 8) led to mob action. In Ephesus, the complaint came from the silversmiths, and it quickly burgeoned into another riot. In a city as large as Ephesus, a riot could be a serious matter.

But in Ephesus, cooler heads prevail, if only barely. In the turmoil of the mob, the Jews of the city "pushed forward" a man named Alexander, who was himself a Jew, probably doing so because they felt he would be a good mediator for the situation. Their instincts were correct, but it did take a while for Alexander to gain control. When the assembled crowd recognized that Alexander was Jewish, the crowd erupted into a nationalist kind of chant—*Great is Artemis of the Ephesians!*—seemingly wanting to reassert the city's religious identity in the face of what they assumed would be Alexander's bias toward Paul. But once they quieted down (after two hours!), Alexander appealed to the city's pride. He told the Ephesians that the city and its temple to Artemis were held in high esteem everywhere and that their reputation was not in danger. "Since these things cannot be denied," he told the crowd in 19:36, "you ought to be quiet and do nothing rash." It was good advice, and fortunate for Paul. Alexander told the crowd to follow their own legal protocols, saying that "the courts are open, and there are proconsuls; let them bring charges there against one another" (19:38). Then Alexander said something particularly savvy: "For we are in danger of being charged with rioting today, since there is no cause that we can give to justify this commotion" (19:40).

In this story, then, the criminal justice system served two different purposes that were in some ways opposed to each other. First, the criminal justice system served as a kind of off-ramp for mob violence in a way it had not done in either Philippi or Thessalonica. Alexander pointed to the courts and the proconsuls as the appropriate places to lodge claims against Paul and his companions, and therefore he pushed back against the urge toward mob violence. In Alexander's view, the Roman justice system could act as a legitimate place to make complaints and as a brake on the kinds of mob violence that might spin out of control. But at the same time, Alexander also used the criminal justice system as a threat, turning the possibility of legal action back on the Ephesians. The crowd had been eager to initiate legal proceedings when it was Paul who would have been put on trial. But when it was themselves in the crosshairs, for rioting without cause, the crowd's enthusiasm suddenly dissipated. This shows that Alexander (and the crowd) understood Roman justice as a tool that could be used against enemies but also as a weapon that could be turned against anyone at any time, with terrifying consequences for anyone caught in its gears. After Alexander reminded members of the crowd that they, too, could end up facing charges before the courts and the proconsuls, the mob quickly dissipated.

Already by this story in the nineteenth chapter, Acts has narrated legal scenes in Jerusalem (twice), Philippi, Thessalonica, and Ephesus. But the heart of Acts' engagement with Roman criminal justice systems is still to come. Beginning in chapter 21 and continuing through chapter 26, Acts follows Paul through an extended and complicated stay inside Roman courts and prisons. Some of this material I consider in the next chapter, so I won't cover it all closely now. But here I want to pay attention to the grand sweep of this six-chapter narrative, specifically to the way Paul became ensnared in a system of justice that refused to let him go free, despite what the individuals involved might have wanted. I also want to draw attention to a few specific moments within the story that betray how Luke asks his readers to understand the failures of criminal justice.

We covered the beginning of Paul's saga in the beginning of this book—how, after returning to Jerusalem after a long journey to the west, Paul accompanied some men to the temple for a ritual of purification to reestablish his Jewish credentials in the eyes of some of his skeptics in Jerusalem. His presence in the temple, though, proved to be provocative and explosive, and Paul ended up caught in a mob of angry people who were trying to harm him. (Paul seems to have had a knack for inciting mobs.) That's when the tribune, Claudius Lysias, intervened to take Paul into what he would later describe—dishonestly, when trying to explain away his behavior to his superior, the governor Felix—as protective custody. When Paul was arrested, "the violence of the mob was so great that he had to be carried by the soldiers," Luke tells us in 21:35, a ferocious crowd indeed. If the crowd really was that intent on harming Paul, then perhaps the actions of the tribune in arresting him were noble after all.

But the next section of Acts seems to anticipate that reaction and heads it off. Having been brought indoors, as he was about to be sent to a holding area, Paul spoke to the tribune in Greek, asking, "May I say something to you?" This, Acts tells us, caught the tribune off guard, as he responded to Paul by asking, rhetorically, whether Paul knew Greek. Then the tribune asked—again probably knowing the answer to his own question—"then you are not the Egyptian who recently stirred up a revolt and led the four thousand assassins out into the wilderness?" (21:38). The tribune likely was referring to a small revolt that happened in the mid-50s, around this same time. This whole exchange reveals that the tribune Claudius Lysias had arrested Paul not because he was trying to protect him and not because he thought that there was merit to the mob's criticisms of Paul, but because the tribune assumed Paul was a criminal.

Race and ethnicity worked differently in the ancient world than they do in our world, but they were still powerful categories that could produce enduring and damaging prejudices. The American view of race began in the period of the Enlightenment in Europe, and the experiences of chattel slavery and the country's more recent debates over who ought to be allowed to immigrate to the United States, honed the particularly American way of thinking about race. Of course, the ancient world had its own forms of bias and prejudice, many of which were based on ethnicity and some of which were even based on skin color. Ancient Roman prejudices didn't work quite the same way our prejudices do, but they were prejudices all the same.

The tribune's assumption that Paul must have been the notorious Egyptian rebel probably rested on some of those ancient Roman prejudices. Romans tended to have a bias against Egyptians, associating them with criminality and assuming that they were disreputable people. That's likely how a figure like that Egyptian rebel became notorious in the first place. In a culture in which Egyptians were thought to be criminals and criminals were thought to be characteristically Egyptian, the news of an Egyptian suspected of doing criminal things would have spread quickly. If Egyptians were criminals and criminals were Egyptians, and if Paul was being hauled up and chased by a mob and accused of criminality, then Paul must be both criminal and Egyptian.

We can easily see these kinds of assumptions working in our own day and time. In President Trump's speech in 2015, announcing his first presidential bid, he used just this kind of ethnic reasoning to talk about immigrants from Mexico. "When Mexico sends its people, they're not sending their best," he said. "... They're sending people that have lots of problems, and they're bringing those problems with us. They're bringing drugs. They're bringing crime. They're rapists. And some, I assume, are good people."[4] Speaking of Haitian immigrants in Springfield, Ohio, and repeating information he had apparently gleaned from a viral right-wing meme, during a 2024 presidential debate Trump claimed that "they are eating the dogs. The people that came in, they are eating the cats. They're eating—they are eating the pets of the people that live there."[5] These comments about Haitian immigrants provoked widespread mockery online and on the political left, but they represent a deeply rooted kind of ethnic and racial bias on the part of both Trump and the right-wing political ecosystem

[4] "Trump Says Lots on Mexico, Whose Leaders Aren't Shy, Either," Associated Press, August 31, 2016, https://apnews.com/article/7d757c5dc4304f348a20623de34349cd.

[5] Mike Catalini, Julie Carr Smyth, and Bruce Shipkowski, "Trump Falsely Accuses Immigrants in Ohio of Abducting and Eating Pets," Associated Press, September 11, 2024, https://apnews.com/article/haitian-immigrants-vance-trump-ohio-6e4a47c52b23ae2c802d216369512ca5.

that spread the meme in the first place. These comments (and many others) reveal the ways Trump and others equate race and ethnicity with criminality and inhumanity. During his first administration he called Haiti and El Salvador and African nations "shithole" countries and wondered aloud why the United States couldn't have more immigrants from Norway.[6] By no means is this kind of behavior confined to Donald Trump; ethnic and racial bias is a longstanding and deeply engrained part of American culture.

The tribune demonstrated the same kind of bias. When confronted with a situation of suspected criminality, Claudius Lysias assumed, with no evidence whatsoever, that an Egyptian must have been responsible. It was only when Paul spoke to him in Greek (which was the common language of commerce and government in the Roman Empire, especially in the east) that the tribune began to suspect that his biases had misled him. After all (the tribune seemed to be thinking), an Egyptian couldn't possibly be well-spoken. If Paul had not spoken up in the tribune's own language, the tribune might never have realized that Paul was not the supposed Egyptian rebel. And even after the tribune learned (in 22:25–26) that Paul claimed Roman citizenship, the tribune's ethnic bias persisted. "It cost me a large sum of money to get my citizenship" (22:28), the tribune told Paul, implying that someone as common and apparently impoverished as Paul must have been lying about being a Roman. Even when presented with substantial evidence that Paul was not the criminal he had assumed him to be, the tribune had a hard time accepting the truth.

This kind of bias shows up frequently in our world today. Think of the experiences of non-White people who are followed around stores by employees on the assumption that they are there to steal something. Or think of the people who have been rounded up by ICE and other law enforcement officers merely on suspicion of being undocumented. Recently, residents of Dearborn, Michigan, who are of Somali descent have begun carrying paperwork proving their citizenship, just in case such an encounter occurs, and others elsewhere have begun to do the same. "They contribute nothing. I don't want them in our country," President Trump recently said of Somali-Americans. "We can go one way or the other, and we're going to go the wrong way, if we keep taking in garbage into our country."[7] Such public statements, including describing Americans—let alone human beings—as "garbage," contribute to the kinds of

[6] Cooper, Jonathan J., "Trump Once Denied Using This Slur Against Haiti and African Nations. Now He Boasts About It," *Associated Press*, December 9, 2025, https://apnews.com/article/trump-slur-haiti-africa-immigration-28aa0785d6f3c68fd4d9e823b6397429.

[7] Aamer Madhani, "Trump Says He Doesn't Want Somalis in the US, Urges Them to Go Back to Their Homeland and Fix It," Associated Press, December 2, 2025, https://apnews.com/article/trump-somalia-immigration-afghanistan-421eaa7ff218c43ccaed3cbab8ed37f5.

racial and ethnic biases and prejudices that have long characterized American society, and they are not so different from the kind of bias that landed Paul in Roman custody and kept him there.

From that point onward in Acts, all the way until the end of the book, Paul was a prisoner of the Roman state. Even by the end of Acts, Paul was never able to get free, though not for lack of trying. In the next chapter we follow Paul during his time in custody, through a series of transfers from one form of detention to the next, as he appeared before one official after another and moved through a system that found him more valuable incarcerated than free.

Living with Unjust Criminal Justice Systems

As the work of Michelle Alexander shows, and as I learned from Harmon Wray all those years ago, America's criminal justice system has never been particularly fair or just. The system as we know it today emerged in the wake of slavery and into the world of Jim Crow, and it has always worked differently for different people based on race, ethnicity, and financial resources. That's not always because individuals within the criminal justice system act in racist or bigoted ways, but because the system itself reflects the deep prejudices built into American society.

The same was true for the Roman world in many ways. Apostles like Paul, John, and Peter repeatedly found themselves caught in various parts of a sprawling and often confusing justice system, in which everyone from governors to magistrates to temple captains to councils to mobs passed judgment and meted out punishments in a web of power. Then as now the system treated different people differently, and then as now the system worked to surveil and profile some people while letting other people skate by with the benefit of the doubt. Faced with such a system, to slip out of tight spots a person like Paul had to rely on a network of friends and allies, the goodwill of individuals within the system, and his own hustle and eloquence. Even then, Paul likely wasn't able to free himself from the Roman criminal justice system. The Book of Acts doesn't tell us what happened to Paul in Rome, but the fact that it *doesn't* tell us probably *does* tell us it was an unhappy ending.

This is a lesson for people who live in a society that weaponizes the criminal justice system and that does not work to ensure that its systems are fair and equitable. In such a society, guilt and innocence do not matter very much, and instead connections, influence, and things like ethnicity and race always matter more. In the United States today, and in other places around the world, criminal justice systems are tools that autocrats can leverage against opponents to silence or sideline them. Trials, courts, and ultimately prisons are a black hole into which authoritarians can send their enemies. A few months after it happened, news broke of a plan hatched by Pentagon officials after two people survived an air strike on their boat in the Caribbean in October of 2025. The plan was to send the men to an infamous El Salvadoran prison.[8] The men could not be allowed to enter the United States to be tried there for the crimes for which their boat was purportedly destroyed, the thinking went, because then their attorneys would have been able to bring evidence that the strikes were illegal. Best to send them to a Salvadoran prison, where they could be held in legal limbo for the rest of their lives, just like Paul. In the end, the men were sent back to their home countries, and in that they were fortunate. In another boat strike that has been made public, when officials (including Defense Secretary Pete Hegseth) saw two survivors clinging to the wreckage of their boat, they simply called in more strikes and kept bombing the boats until the men were dead.

Meanwhile, mere hours after being inaugurated, one of President Trump's first acts when he returned to office for a second term was to grant pardons to over 1,500 people who had been tried and convicted of participating in the insurrection at the U.S. Capitol building on January 6, 2021.[9] Included in the pardons were hundreds of people who had been accused and convicted of assault and obstructing law enforcement. At the same time, Trump ordered that any pending charges against other January 6 rioters be dropped. The juxtaposition between those pardons, the ongoing roundups of people wrongly suspected of being in the United States illegally, and the extrajudicial killings in the Caribbean boat strikes make something clear: in the United States, justice works differently for different people, depending on race and ethnicity and proximity to power. In that, as a country we are not so different from the Roman Empire.

Further Reading

If you are interested in an insider's view of one corner of the American criminal justice system, including some discussion of my old teacher Harmon Wray, Preston Shipp's book *Confessions of a Former Prosecutor* is a great choice.[10] And I'll draw attention again to Michelle Alexander's work as a forceful and

[8] Damien Cave, Edward Wong, and Maria Abi-Habib, "Inside the Pentagon's Scramble to Deal with Boat Strike Survivors," *New York Times*, December 9, 2025, https://www.nytimes.com/2025/12/09/us/politics/pentagon-boat-strike-survivors.html?searchResultPosition=1.

[9] Max Matza, "Proud Boys and Oath Keepers among over 1,500 Capitol Riot Defendants Pardoned by Trump," *BBC News*, January 20, 2025, https://www.bbc.com/news/articles/c5y7l47xrpko.

[10] Preston Shippwith and Eric Wilson, *Confessions of a Former Prosecutor: Abandoning Vengeance and Embracing True Justice* (Chalice Press, 2024).

overwhelming argument about the racial biases embedded in American systems of justice.

In this chapter I mentioned the differences between ancient and modern concepts of race and ethnicity. Denise Kimber Buell has done marvelous work on ancient understandings of bias, and her chapter "God's Own People" in the book *Prejudice and Christian Beginnings* is a good place to start.[11] In fact, that whole book is full of wonderful work by many different scholars. Buell's book *Why This New Race: Ethnic Reasoning in Early Christianity* is a classic and well worth your time. If you are interested in tracing the ways Christian theological traditions are entangled with ideas of race, J. Kameron Carter's book *Race: A Theological Account* is wonderful,[12] as is the work of my colleague Ted Vial in his book *Modern Race, Modern Religion.*[13] And if you are interested in exploring modern American ways of thinking about race and systems of racism, some of my favorites are *Between the World and Me* by Ta-Nehisi Coates,[14] *Racecraft* by Barbara and Karen Fields,[15] and *The Fire Next Time* by James Baldwin.[16]

[11] Denise Kimber Buell, "God's Own People: Specters of Race, Ethnicity, and Gender in Early Christian Studies," in *Prejudice and Christian Beginnings: Investigating Race, Gender, and Ethnicity in Early Christian Studies* (Fortress Press, 2009).

[12] J. Kameron Carter, *Race: A Theological Account* (Oxford University Press, 2008).

[13] Theodore Vial, *Modern Religion, Modern Race* (Oxford University Press, 2016).

[14] Ta-Nehisi Coates, *Between the World and Me* (Spiegel & Grau, 2015).

[15] Karen E. Fields and Barbara J. Fields, *Racecraft: The Soul of Inequality in American Life* (Verso, 2012).2012

[16] James Baldwin, *The Fire Next Time* (Vintage, 1992).

6

Imprisonment

In mid-July of 2025, I stopped at a grocery store in rural eastern Tennessee to buy snacks for a long road trip all the way back to Colorado. The place had only one real store, so I pulled into the parking lot on the way out of town. I grabbed all the stuff that would keep me fed and entertained across the Midwest and the high plains—chips and candy and a cooler full of ice and drinks. As I walked up to the only open checkout lane, I noticed the T-shirt on the man in front of me. In big block letters, his shirt read: "MAKE ALLIGATORS GREAT AGAIN." That's all it said.

I had spent the summer in the middle of the woods, immersed in an intensive writing program, so I hadn't been following the news as closely as I often do. But standing there in the checkout line, I began to piece things together. The man's shirt was riffing on Donald Trump's campaign slogan, "Make America Great Again," so I knew it had to be related to politics somehow. And I remembered the recent announcement, only a few weeks earlier, of a site in Florida that they were calling Alligator Alcatraz. Florida had announced the facility in June, and by the first of July, Donald Trump was already touring it. It was a prison—euphemistically called an immigration detention facility—located in the swamps of South Florida. The state of Florida runs Alligator Alcatraz, but it housed federal prisoners who had been rounded up as part of immigration raids.

The facility's nickname and the man's T-shirt referred to the prison's location in Florida's swamps. The idea—as many conservative commentators gleefully pointed out—was that the prison would be extra secure because anyone who escaped would immediately face attack by the swamp's numerous and sizeable alligators. The call to "MAKE ALLIGATORS GREAT AGAIN" was an expression of a desire—a fantasy—that wild animals would attack and eat some of the people who would be imprisoned there. It wouldn't be enough for migrants to be arrested and imprisoned, often for months on end, without access to attorneys or legal services or even clear information about what kinds of charges they were facing. It wasn't enough to turn back people at the U.S. border. The man wearing the T-shirt—and the president of the United States and many of his supporters—wanted migrants to suffer and die.

Several years earlier I met a woman I'll call Maria. Before I met her, Maria had been living in Mexico with her family, and she had had a food cart from which she sold meals every afternoon. One day a drug cartel came to her cart, kicked it over and spilled its contents everywhere, and told her she would need to begin paying them protection money to keep something bad from happening to her. Maria had seen the same thing done to other people, and she knew what would occur if she ignored them or tried to avoid paying the cartel. They would kill her, she felt sure, or they would hurt her or harm her children. Maria knew other people who had experienced the same thing, and she had seen the terrible things that happened to people who defied the cartels. And she knew this from firsthand experience, too; Maria's own husband was already sitting in prison. He had been arrested after a cartel called in a favor to the local authorities and had him locked up. She wasn't quite sure what he had done, and her husband wouldn't say, but he had somehow gotten crossways with one of the cartels, and they had made sure he would stay locked away in jail. As far as I know, he's still there today.

Maria considered her options. She could pay the cartel money she didn't have. She could take a chance on defying them and risk certain harm to herself or her children. Or Maria could flee. She chose to run. In the fall of 2018, Maria headed north toward Mexico's border with the United States, and she crossed over into Arizona, where she hoped to find work and bring her children to live with her. But ICE arrested her shortly after she crossed, and Maria ended up spending months in an ICE facility in Arizona. She remembers that she was questioned frequently by ICE agents in rapid bursts and that the agents acted impatient and ended their sessions abruptly when they didn't like what she was saying. The agents had never told Maria why she had been arrested, how long she could expect to be there, or what she could do to plead her case. And they had not told her about her legal right to request extra time to respond to the agents' questions. So she endured their aggressive questioning, and whenever they stormed off she went back into the ICE prison to wait. After several months in Arizona, without explanation Maria was transferred to another ICE facility in Aurora, Colorado, near my home. She liked the Colorado facility a little better because she was able to spend a few moments outdoors there—something she had never been able to do in Arizona.

While she was imprisoned in ICE facilities, Maria had no way to contact her family, and her kids didn't know where she was. She disappeared into the system. It was only after several months in the Colorado facility that Maria had a stroke of luck. A local attorney took her case pro bono, and together they began the legal proceedings that would help her seek asylum. Maria feels sure that, without that attorney, she would have been deported back to Mexico and likely to her death. The attorney helped Maria find a local Colorado family who would vouch for her and offer to support her while she filed her asylum case, which allowed her to be released from custody. That family—who were strangers to her—took her in and provided for her needs. Eventually Maria's children were able to join her in the United States, but even now, a half-dozen years later, Maria's case is still pending.

Maria crossed the border into the United States and was arrested and imprisoned during the first Trump Administration, but if anything conditions have only gotten worse for people seeking asylum since then. While Maria felt lost and abandoned within the immigration system, at least she was a part of a system, dysfunctional and cruel as it was. Others, now, face far harsher circumstances. The United States now is imprisoning people indefinitely or deporting them without due process, making an already bad system far crueler and more arbitrary. The United States has sold some immigrants into imprisonment in other countries, such as El Salvador, where they face a lifetime of imprisonment in horrific circumstances without much hope of release, and they have deported others to war-torn nations that are not their own countries of origin, where they face uncertain futures. And on the American right, people print T-shirts that read "MAKE ALLIGATORS GREAT AGAIN" and wear them to the grocery store, delighting in the possibility that people like Maria might end up in a prison in a swamp somewhere, hunted like prey by alligators and ICE agents alike. To some Americans caught up in the nationalist frenzy of "securing the border," being an immigrant or even being *suspected* of being an immigrant is enough for someone to deserve indefinite imprisonment or death.

How Does Imprisonment Work?

In the previous chapter we looked at the American and Roman criminal justice systems, and we noticed how such systems are not always devoted to actual criminal justice. Instead, criminal justice systems often reflect society's deep prejudices and subject different people to different experiences based on their race, ethnicity, or ability to afford an attorney. Imprisonment, or incarceration, is an integral part of modern criminal justice systems, and experiences of imprisonment reflect the same biases and prejudices as the rest of the systems do. In the United States, we are living in an *age of mass incarceration*. According to The Sentencing Project, an advocacy and research group that focuses on justice, "over five million people in total are under supervision by the criminal legal system" in the United States currently, and "two million people, disproportionately Black, are living in prisons and jails instead of their communities."[1] In the current age of American mass incarceration, they go on to point out, the American incarceration rate far exceeds the rates of most other countries, and it is dramatically higher than the incarceration rate in the United States at other times in its history. American prisons are swollen with people who ran afoul of "three strikes and you're out" laws, the so-called "War on Drugs," and mandatory sentencing requirements. American prison populations grew especially quickly in the 1980s and 1990s, as being "tough on crime" became a calling card for many politicians seeking office.

There's a tension in the way we talk about imprisonment. Sometimes we think of prison as a means of punishment, and sometimes we think of it as a means of rehabilitation. One of the earliest American experiments in incarceration was the Eastern State Penitentiary, which opened in 1829 in Philadelphia.[2] Eastern State was a new model of prison, a *penitentiary*—a word that comes from same root as the religious words *penance* or *penitence*. Religiously speaking, to be penitent or to do penance is to reflect on one's wrongdoing and to offer recompense or seek reconciliation for it. At the Eastern State Penitentiary inmates lived alone, and they were supposed to devote their time to reflecting on their wrongdoing; it was a place designed for doing the work of penance. Each room contained an opening in the ceiling through which inmates could see the sky, which was called the "eye of God." The implication was that as the prisoners engaged in contemplation and penitence, God would be watching them. The design of Eastern State Penitentiary suggested a focus on rehabilitation, but there was plenty of room for punishment too. The prison included a form of solitary confinement in which prisoners could be held without contact from other people, something that has become very common in American prisons. And various harsh forms of physical punishment were used to control inmates who ran afoul of the penitentiary's rules.

The Eastern State Penitentiary has been closed for decades, and the building now functions as a museum. But its legacy can be felt across the American prison system. The tension between rehabilitation and punishment has only intensified with time. As prison populations swelled in the late twentieth century, programs for inmates to engage in self-improvement shrank. And as more and more prisoners received longer sentences and sentencing guidelines

---

[1] "Mass Incarceration Trends," The Sentencing Project, 2024, https://www.sentencingproject.org/reports/mass-incarceration-trends/.

[2] For a wonderful essay that includes information on Eastern State, see Jonathan Gleason, "Proxemics," *Colorado Review* 50, no. 1 (2023): 35–48, https://dx.doi.org/10.1353/col.2023.0009.

removed the possibility of parole for many, the idea of rehabilitation (in which prisoners were working toward reintegration with society) faded away. Today, American prisons are filled with long-term inmates who probably should have been released years ago but who are kept in prison because releasing them would be politically dangerous for the politicians who would have to pass the laws to release them.

Some prisoners and prisoner activists point out the special injustice of keeping people incarcerated for actions involving things (like using marijuana) that have since become legal or have been decriminalized. It is unjust to continue to imprison someone for selling an ounce of marijuana twenty years ago, many prisoners and advocates claim, while people can currently open a dispensary a couple of doors down from a Starbucks. But despite Jesus' promise in Luke 4 to "proclaim release to the captives," not many elections have been won on that platform, and it's easy to gain public office by promising to be tough on crime. So America's prisons continue to be overcrowded.

Ancient incarceration worked a little differently. For years, scholars have claimed that prisons as we know them are a late invention, that modern prisons came into existence only recently. In that way of thinking, ancient prisons were more like modern jails: holding spaces for people who were awaiting trial, not long-term punishment for crime. But the recent research of scholars like Matthew D.C. Larsen and Mark Letteney has shown that prisons existed in the ancient world too as places where inmates might be held for long periods of time.[3] Nonetheless, ancient incarceration was not quite the same as modern incarceration. Today, prison represents a substantial commitment on the part of federal, state, and local government budgets, and new facilities—like the so-called Alligator Alcatraz—are often lauded as important public utilities and celebrated by the politicians who brought them into existence. The ancient world imprisoned a far smaller proportion of the population, and often it was for shorter periods of time until some other punishment could be determined.

The latter chapter of Acts, as we have seen, offers us a tour of the ancient Roman criminal justice system. Although Luke does not bring us into any intimate scenes from inside a prison, we do get glimpses of Paul's experiences of incarceration and how his life and his imprisonment became assets in the political careers of others in ways that mirror the experiences of people incarcerated in the United States today. Once Acts tells the story of Paul entering the Roman justice system, once the tribune Claudius Lysias takes him into custody in Jerusalem, Luke never shows us Paul living free again.

[3] Matthew D.C. Larsen and Mark Letteney, *Ancient Mediterranean Incarceration* (University of California Press, 2025).

That experience is familiar and common to hundreds of thousands of people today—people whose lives have become points scored by politicians and whose freedom has become subject to someone else's cruelty.

Paul's Imprisonment in Acts

It is ironic that Claudius Lysias wrote in his letter to the governor Felix (in Acts 23:26–30) that he had "rescued" Paul and brought him to safety—because Paul's safety was severely compromised by the simple act of the tribune taking him into custody. When Paul had been a free person, there had been several plots against him already, as Acts 9:23–25, 9:29–30, 20:3, and 20:19 attest. He escaped those planned attacks by slipping away quietly and being willing to move quickly to a new place. But once he was in custody, Paul became less safe because his movements became more predictable and his location was better known. In Acts 23:12–23, Luke tells of a plot against Paul by "the Jews," an undefined and amorphous group that presumably had some relationship to the people who had sought Paul in the Temple earlier.

The plot against Paul seems to have been quite serious, as the conspirators pledged not to eat or drink until they had killed Paul. They proposed to "the chief priests and elders" that those officials should ask the Roman authorities to be allowed to make another examination of Paul so they could ensure that he would be transferred to the venue of the hearing. Along the way, the plan went, as Paul was being transferred, they would attack and kill Paul. Whether this particular plot against Paul was historical or not, or whether Luke's repeated references to schemes against Paul's life were just several different reflections of the same general sentiment that many people didn't seem to like the guy, is not clear. And it's possible that Luke was using the apparently widespread dislike for Paul to ratchet up the tension in the story and to highlight the differences between Paul and other Jewish folks in Jerusalem. But if the plot was real, and even if there was no specific threat against Paul, putting him in prison was hardly good for his safety and well-being, as most people who have spent time incarcerated can tell you. In prison, even in the comparatively comfortable kinds of confinement that Paul apparently sometimes experienced, freedom is constrained and one's ability to escape attack is reduced. For someone like Paul, who was used to slipping away from trouble and skipping town when things went wrong, prison must have felt especially constraining, like he suddenly had nowhere to hide and he was at the mercy of the people seeking him out. Claudius Lysias, if Luke's account is accurate, took seriously the report of a plot. He ordered two centurions to accompany Paul on his journey to see the governor Felix in Caesarea, equipped them with two hundred soldiers, seventy horsemen, and two hundred spearmen, and ordered the centurions to give Paul a horse to ride. Such a strong show of military strength suggests that Paul was a big target and that—once the tribune had heard Paul was a Roman citizen—he wanted to protect Paul from harm.

With such a robust escort, Paul made it safely to Felix in the city of Caesarea. Felix was the governor (or procurator) of the province of Judea. As governor, Felix would have been the highest authority in the province, answerable to the emperor in Rome. Felix received Paul into custody, and in Acts 23:35 he ordered Paul to be held under guard in "Herod's headquarters," which was the *praetorium*—the place where a regional government did its work. Such a building would have included some cells for holding prisoners just like Paul as they waited for their cases to be handled. Acts specifies that five days passed before Felix began to hear Paul's case and that some of Paul's accusers came to Caesarea to make their arguments against him. In a trial scene that stretches from 24:1 to 24:23, the high priest Ananias (who was high priest beginning in the year 48), some other Jewish elders, and an attorney named Tertullus presented their case against Paul, and Paul presented his defense. But at the end of the hearing Felix did not feel that he had learned enough, and in 24:22 he put off deciding the case until Claudius Lysias could join the proceedings. Then in another description of how Paul was held prisoner, 24:23 says that Felix "ordered the centurion to keep him in custody, but to let him have some liberty and not to prevent any of his friends from taking care of his needs." Like the earlier five-day imprisonment in the praetorium, this seems to have been a relatively comfortable form of incarceration, and Paul was able to maintain some of his freedom and well-being through the support of his friends, who were allowed to bring him food and other comfort items. Here we see incarceration not as punishment, but simply as a waystation as a trial was unfolding. Paul might have been frustrated by his confinement, but things could have been a lot worse.

But things did get worse for Paul—and quickly. In 24:26–27, Luke tells us that Felix never did send for Claudius Lysias to decide Paul's case as he had said he would. Instead, Felix began to think of Paul and his imprisonment differently, not in terms of delivering justice but as a kind of financial and political asset:

> At the same time [writes Luke] he hoped that money would be given him by Paul, and for that reason he used to send for him very often and converse with him. After two years had passed, Felix was succeeded by Porcius Festus, and since he wanted to grant the Jews a favor, Felix left Paul in prison.

Felix, who should have decided the case against Paul and either remanded Paul for punishment or set him free, instead prolonged Paul's confinement in hopes of receiving a bribe.

This is a stunning detail for Luke to have included. In several places in his narratives, both in the Gospel of Luke and in Acts, Luke portrays Roman officials in an unflattering light. Some of them look gutless, and others of them seem disinterested in their work. Generally speaking, Luke does not puff up Roman officials, and his assessments of them tend to be honest. But this goes further than mere honesty. Here, Luke portrays Felix—who is, let's remind ourselves, *the governor of a Roman province*—as actively on the take. Thinking back to the introduction of this book, and some of the theories about who Luke might have been and what kind of a relationship the dedication to "most excellent Theophilus" might have represented, Luke's description of Felix's conduct in 24:26–27 is a shocking accusation. If Theophilus was in fact a "most excellent" imperial official (notice how the Greek word that is being translated as "most excellent" in Luke's dedication to Theophilus in Luke 1:3 is the same word being translated as "his Excellency" in Acts 23:26, in Claudius Lysias' letter to Felix), then Luke's description of Felix's actions amounted to a denouncement of one of Theophilus' colleagues and a serious charge against the whole Roman system of government.

Felix committed two acts that should strike us as immoral, but neither one would probably surprise anyone familiar with the workings of criminal justice systems. First, Felix prolonged Paul's imprisonment (by delaying the conclusion of his hearing) because the governor was seeking a bribe—because the longer Paul was in prison, the more benefit accrued to the person in charge of the case. Felix hoped that the longer Paul sat in prison without the ability to continue with his life, the more willing he might become to raise some funds to pay Felix to let him go. Bribery of this kind tends to be rare in functional governments, where public servants face accountability and systems usually work transparently. But in autocratic systems—which put the authority and whims of a leader and that leader's political party at the center of things—bribery quickly becomes endemic.

Here, it's important to think about Felix himself and how he ended up in his position as governor. Felix likely did not choose government as a career from among many other options, training for the role and working his way up through a series of lower administrative roles until he became governor on the merits of his performance. And he certainly was not elected to the role. Instead, Felix likely landed the job of governor because of his affiliations with the emperor and because his social class—his family of origin and his economic status—dictated that he was the kind of person who ought to be rewarded with such a position. If he was anything like the kinds of people who often end up in such jobs in authoritarian and autocratic regimes, then Felix would not have held a principled view of his work and his position: he would have viewed it as a vehicle for his own personal advancement.

Tom Homan—the so-called "border czar" of the second Trump Administration—is the person charged with coordinating and facilitating the United States' campaign against undocumented immigrants. Homan had been acting ICE director during the first Trump Administration and was a frequent voice in media, calling for tightened borders and deportation. "Tom Homan will be in charge of all Deportation of Illegal Aliens back to their Country of Origin," Trump wrote in a Truth Social post, with idiosyncratic capitalization, adding that "there is nobody better at policing and controlling our borders."[4] As border czar, Homan has presided over a rapid expansion of ICE prison facilities, with dozens of new detention centers opening in the first year of the new presidential term. Although places like Alligator Alcatraz get a lot of media attention, similar prisons (without the alligators) have been opening all over the country.

But in 2024, in the lead-up to the presidential election, Homan accepted a bag of cash from an undercover FBI agent, according to numerous reports.[5] The FBI sting was part of an investigation into broader national security matters. According to the sources who publicized the sting, Homan agreed to fix the awarding of government contracts related to immigration—the kind of work he had done in the first Trump Administration and was poised to take up again in the second Trump Administration—in exchange for a bag filled with fifty thousand dollars. This is bribery pure and simple. If the allegations are true, instead of pursuing and administering immigration policy in the best interest of the people, Homan agreed to steer contracts toward the people who had paid him the bribe. The FBI's investigation was ongoing when the presidential transition took place in January of 2025, and in the summer of 2025—around the time many new ICE facilities were being opened, including Alligator Alcatraz—Trump's FBI director, Kash Patel, closed the investigation. A statement said that the investigation had found no wrongdoing.[6]

---

[4] Rachel Treisman, "What to Know about Tom Homan, the Former ICE Head Returning as Trump's 'Border Czar,'" NPR, November 11, 2024, https://www.npr.org/2024/11/11/nx-s1-5186522/tom-homan-border-czar-trump.

[5] Devlin Barrett et al., "Trump Justice Dept. Closed Investigation into Tom Homan for Accepting Bag of Cash," *New York Times*, September 20, 2025, https://www.nytimes.com/2025/09/20/us/politics/tom-homan-fbi-trump.html.

[6] Sarah N. Lynch, "Trump Aide Homan Accepted $50,000 in Bribery Sting Operation, Sources Say," Reuters, September 22, 2025, https://www.reuters.com/world/us/trump-aide-homan-accepted-50000-bribery-sting-operation-sources-say-2025-09-21/.

Similar to how Felix used his position to try to squeeze a bribe out of Paul, if the allegations are true, then Homan used his once-and-future position to squeeze a bribe out of the people who wanted to receive large government contracts. Since the investigation was closed, there may be no way to know whether the bag full of cash did end up influencing the awarding of government contracts, but the OBBBA (the "One Big Beautiful Bill Act") appropriated forty-five billion dollars to expand prisons for immigrants and quadrupled the annual ICE detention budget. With all that federal cash washing around, plenty of companies were able to see their investments pay off.

That was the first of Felix's acts that should strike us as immoral—seeking a bribe to let a prisoner go free. But the second immoral act was just as bad, and potentially worse. "After two years had passed," Acts 24:27 reads, "Felix was succeeded by Porcius Festus, and since he wanted to grant the Jews a favor, Felix left Paul in prison." Since he couldn't get a bribe out of Paul (who, I suspect, simply didn't have the resources to offer one), Felix decided to keep Paul detained as an asset of a different kind, namely as a way to settle a political debt. We don't know what kind of favors Felix might have owed or whether Paul's continued detention would have been welcome news to "the Jews" (likely the people who had first pursued Paul in the temple two years earlier—Ananias and others) or not. But Felix's casual abandonment of Paul as he rotated out of his post as governor represented a dereliction of his specific duty to judge the cases that came before him, and it also represented a breach of a broader duty to administer justice in the province.

It didn't take long for the new governor Festus to take up Paul's case. Acts 25 begins with the news that Paul's accusers were still very keen to have him convicted, and they were quick to try to win Festus to their side. For his part, Festus agreed to hear the case in Caesarea soon, and he invited anyone who wanted to accuse Paul to show up there. This is how Paul's case initially proceeded—and should have kept on proceeding—under Felix. From Paul's perspective, this had to have been exasperating; he was beginning the judicial process all over again. But then Festus showed, in the same way Felix had before, that the criminal justice system and Paul's confinement within it were not about justice at all. "But Festus," Acts 25:9 reports, "wishing to do the Jews a favor, asked Paul, 'Do you wish to go up to Jerusalem and be tried there before me on these charges?" Paul sensed a trap, and he realized (probably correctly) that a change of venue would put the trial back on the home turf of his accusers and expose him to more acts of targeted violence. "I am standing before the emperor's tribunal," he replied, and "this is where I should be tried. I have done no wrong to the Jews, as you very well know" (25:10). The irritation is evident in Paul's words, and the narrator's remark that Festus was "wishing to do the Jews a favor" seems accurate. Festus was trying to sell out Paul by moving his trial to Jerusalem, where the attitudes against Paul were most inflamed, even when there was no justification for it. Paul refused. "I appeal to the emperor," Paul announced in 25:11. After Festus talked it over with his advisors, he agreed.

Paul's experiences in Roman custody in Caesarea were a confusing nightmare of unclear procedures, ambivalent and hostile officials, and endless detention. I am reminded of Maria's story of detention in ICE facilities—how she never had any sense of what she could do to get free from detention, how she could even begin the process, or what her rights might have been. And I am reminded of the experiences of many others in prisons in the United States and elsewhere—people who are held long after their debt to society has been paid (if one was ever owed at all) because it is more politically expedient for someone to keep them in prison than to set them free. The way Luke tells the story, Paul's experiences in the Roman prison system included more than one instance of someone trading on his captivity—someone in a position of power attempting to leverage Paul's imprisonment for personal enrichment. Both Felix and Festus sought to profit from Paul's incarceration, either directly or indirectly. It was perhaps not as straightforward a scheme as accepting a bag full of cash in exchange for steering government prison contracts, but the corruption of Felix and Festus was nevertheless brazen.

Following an interesting interlude featuring Paul's interactions with Agrippa and Bernice—siblings, children of Herod Agrippa, who were long rumored to have been in a romantic relationship with each other—Paul began his journey to receive his audience with the emperor. This journey as it is told in Acts has echoes of Homer's Odyssey and all the elements of a thrilling sea story, but we should also recognize it as an extension of Paul's time in imperial detention. Though he was not in a prison while he was crossing the Mediterranean on his way to Rome, neither was Paul free. In 27:1, Luke tells us that Paul "and some other prisoners" were put into the custody of a Julius, who was a centurion of the Augustan Cohort, and they embarked on first one ship and then another. A number of adventures ensued, including a dramatic shipwreck on the island of Malta late in chapter 27. There, in Malta, they overwintered then resumed their journey in the spring.

The final phase of Paul's imprisonment (the final phase that Luke tells us about, anyway) comes in chapter 28 of Acts. Here, we learn that "Paul was allowed to live by himself, with the soldier who was guarding him" (28:16), and Acts tells of how Paul hosted members of the Jewish diaspora community in Rome and held discussions with them. "He lived there two whole years at his own expense," the final verses of the Book of Acts report, "and welcomed all who came to him, proclaiming the kingdom of God and teaching about the Lord Jesus Christ with all boldness and without hindrance" (28:30–31). Again, though Paul's confinement was comfortable by the standards of imprisonment, he was not free. At this point, it was approaching five years since he had been taken into protective custody by the tribune Claudius Lysias in the Jerusalem temple, and despite having spent all that time in Roman custody, Paul was still captive to the empire. Paul was still not free.

Living in an Age of Incarceration

Though Luke does not tell us what happened to Paul at the end of his five-year imprisonment by the Roman Empire, local tradition in Rome has it that he was executed there. If that is true, then Paul spent the last years of his life incarcerated, seeking his freedom the whole time, and he never managed to escape the system that had first arrested him purportedly for his own protection. Paul died trying to get free.

In that regard, Paul's story reflects the experiences of many people who are caught in systems of incarceration around the world today. People like Maria are stuck in prisons of various kinds, without clear paths to gain their freedom, because imprisoning people is more politically expedient than setting them free—and, often, because prisons are profitable. In the United States especially, incarceration has increased dramatically across the presidential administrations of both parties. And the Trump Administration's immigration efforts have led to expansions of prison facilities and a kind of glee among Trump's supporters about the prospect of condemning immigrants to dangerous and inhumane imprisonment. Meanwhile, figures like Tom Homan are accused of taking bribes to perpetuate the immigration prison system, and many people and corporations profit directly from the expansion of detention centers.

When incarceration is a political expedience rather than an instrument of justice, the system has become warped and unjust. In such a broken system—which breaks more easily and disproportionately in autocratic or authoritarian governments—it can feel hopeless to try to push back. People can feel powerless in the face of such obvious injustice, just as Paul probably did. In such times, one of the best forms of resistance is refusal to equate incarceration with justice—a denial that prison is in itself some kind of civic good. When faced with unjust practices of incarceration, people must pay attention to the ways the criminal justice system is being weaponized against political enemies and monetized by political insiders and the ways people's lives are being used—like Paul's life was used—as assets to be traded and stashed away. In short, the best way to resist unjust incarceration is to become aware of how imprisonment itself is a means and not an end—a means to gaining and maintaining power and a way of inflicting cruelty. In such systems, cruelty can be the point—as the man in the "ALLIGATOR ALCATRAZ" shirt could surely attest.

Further Reading

Mark Letteney and Matthew D.C. Larsen have written perhaps the most exciting new book in recent memory on the subject of ancient prisons. I already cited *Ancient Mediterranean Incarceration* in this chapter, but if you are curious to learn more about how incarceration worked in the ancient world, you should check it out.[7] As an added bonus, the book is available in Open Access, which means you can download and read it for free. A related book—focused more on another of Paul's experiences of imprisonment, but relevant just the same—comes from Ryan Schellenberg. *Abject Joy: Paul, Prison, and the Art of Making Do* follows Paul's imprisonment in Philippi as described in the New Testament text Philippians.[8]

If you are interested in the topic of modern incarceration, I will reiterate my recommendation of *The New Jim Crow* by Michelle Alexander[9] and *Confessions of a Former Prosecutor* by Preston Shipp.[10] And for a radical and bracing take on modern American incarceration—one that's still compelling more than two decades after it was published—Angela Davis' book *Are Prisons Obsolete?* is always a good choice.[11]

---

[7] Larsen and Letteney, *Ancient Mediterranean Incarceration.*

[8] Ryan S. Schellenberg, *Abject Joy: Paul, Prison, and the Art of Making Do*, 1st ed. (Oxford University Press, 2021), https://doi.org/10.1093/oso/9780190065515.001.0001.

[9] Michelle Alexander, *The New Jim Crow: Mass Incarceration in the Age of Colorblindness* (The New Press, 2012).

[10] Preston Shiff with Eric Wilson, *Confessions of a Former Prosecutor: Abandoning Vengeance and Embracing True Justice* (Chalice Press, 2024).

[11] Angela Y. Davis, *Are Prisons Obsolete?* (Seven Stories Press, 2003).

7

Violence

Early in the summer when I was eleven years old, the evening news in our living room was filled with grainy images from China. It was not long after Ferdinand Marcos had resigned as president of the Philippines, and those few years of watching Tom Brokaw on the news every night had helped me become a little more informed about the world. I had seen worldwide crises unfold on our black-and-white television screen—events like the machinations of the late Cold War and Black Monday on the stock market. I was beginning to understand that the wide world was often filled with crises and dramatic stories. But nothing had prepared me for what was happening in Tiananmen Square.

The iconic image from Tiananmen Square that summer was a photograph of a student standing in front of a line of tanks, daring them to run him over. The man looked impossibly small standing in front of such an array of war machinery, and it was easy to imagine the tanks simply moving forward and crushing the man under their treads. But the tanks stood still. It was a shocking image then and visceral in its portrayal of the scale and the stakes of the moment. To this day, no one knows for certain who the man was or what he was trying to accomplish when he stepped in front of the line of tanks. But for me and many people my age, the man became a symbol of the courage required to stand up to state violence.

The protests that came to a head in Tiananmen Square in 1989 began, as many protests do, with young people. That spring, students began to agitate for a range of improvements to their lives. The students didn't really have a unified platform, but they had a list of grievances that varied depending on the person. Some of the students were dissatisfied with their economic prospects at a time when jobs were hard to come by, and some students felt unprepared by their education to enter such a difficult search for employment. Other students were interested in lofty ideals like freedom of speech or civil rights. Together, the students captured something of the zeitgeist of a country in transition—a China that could be repressive in its denials of human rights but that was beginning to enter the world economy in earnest. The students who took part in the protests were anxious about their places in a world and in a China that were both rapidly evolving. And they were frustrated by what they saw as the reluctance of their government to respond to their concerns and the slow pace of change in China compared to everywhere else. After the death of a former pro-reform government official in April, students began to gather to memorialize him, and the gatherings soon grew and morphed into a broader critique of the government. At their height, a million people joined the protests. I remember watching the news and hearing reporters wonder aloud what the Chinese government would do. The movement seemed audacious and provocative for a country that liked to keep a tight lid on dissent. Many of the nightly reports made a point of saying that the Chinese government would not let things go on like that forever.

Those predictions came true when the government declared martial law in May and deployed the military to the place where the protesters were gathering. By early June, the government began to clear the spaces where the students had gathered and violently suppress the protests. On the night of June 3, troops fired first tear gas and rubber bullets into the crowd and then, shockingly, live ammunition. The protesters responded by throwing rocks and Molotov cocktails. Clashes continued into the next day, but it wasn't long before the Chinese military regained control of the space the students had been occupying, a large open space in Beijing called Tiananmen Square. There are no official statistics on the dead and wounded, but estimates range from hundreds to thousands dead and thousands more wounded.

Sitting in our living room in North Carolina, watching video of wounded protestors and stone-faced soldiers and seeing the image of the man standing in front of the column of tanks, I felt a strange mixture of admiration and fear. The admiration came from the fact that I had never seen anyone act as bravely as the million protestors who had put their lives on the line, symbolized so well in the man who had stopped the column of tanks simply by standing in front of them. And the fear came from the realization that such a thing was possible—that a government might turn its guns and its tanks on ordinary people and that the struggle for basic rights and opportunities could move so quickly into violence and death. I took comfort, at the age of eleven, in the naïve idea that such a thing could only happen in a place like China, that the government of my own country would never turn its weapons on its people that way.

The only reason I could feel comforted by the idea that the kind of thing happening in Tiananmen Square could not happen in the United States is that I was too young to remember the Civil Rights Movement and Vietnam protests that had taken place only a decade or two earlier. I had been born at the end of the 1970s, just after the Vietnam War ended and after the most intense periods of the civil rights era. If I had been a bit older (or if those enormous social movements had reached the curricula of my rural Southern schools), I might have known that my confidence was misplaced. (I grew up about twenty miles from the Woolworth's lunch counters where sit-ins had marked a major turning point in the Civil Rights Movement, but I never heard about those sit-ins until high school.) To be sure, the scale of what was happening in Tiananmen Square was larger than anything that had happened in any single event in the United States. But my nation's own recent history was filled with examples of state violence that were no different in kind and degree than what was happening in China. Only the proportions were different. From the shootings at Kent State to the police violence against marchers on the Edmund Pettus Bridge in Selma to the bloody Freedom Summer of 1964, the United States—in my parents' lifetimes—had turned weapons against its own people. Just as in China and in other places around the world, the United States government had resorted to violence, and would do so again, to mark the limits of protest and activism. Although we don't often think of it this way, violence is one of the ways a government keeps its people in line and pushes back when it thinks they have gone too far—when they have become too disruptive in their search for rights, their complaints about the conditions of their lives, or their critique of the government's actions. When a government turns weapons against its own people, we call that state violence.

State Violence

Political scientists often point out that states prefer to monopolize violence. That is, from the perspective of a government, only the state itself should control the means of violence, and neither its external enemies nor its citizens or subjects should be allowed to challenge the state's authority through violence. In most societies, regular people give up some or all of their right to use violence individually; it's a crime in most places to kill someone with whom you're engaging in an argument or to stockpile assault weapons. (The United States represents notable exceptions on both fronts). In exchange, the state promises to use violence on behalf of individuals by employing police who can use force to stop crime, by maintaining a national defense to stop aggression by another country, and by limiting other individuals who might cause someone harm. This is one of the essential bargains of society: we trade our individual violence for collective violence on the assumption and the promise that the violence will be used against others on our behalf and that we will be safer for it.

This arrangement mostly works wonderfully well. Nations that ban or severely restrict the ownership of guns, for example, see far lower rates of murders perpetrated with guns, as you would expect. In such countries, it is often the case that not even the police carry firearms because there is simply less need to do so. Citizens of free and democratic societies that place limits on individual violence usually end up far safer than their counterparts in countries (like the United States) that allow individuals to own weapons, and where police are armed to the teeth, because any traffic stop can turn into a shooting match. But even in the United States, we don't depend on ourselves individually to guarantee our own protection. Even someone with an assault rifle doesn't stand much of a chance against an invading army or a hostile neighbor intent on causing harm. Instead, we place our trust in our government to provide security and to use violence on our behalf when necessary.

State violence, say political scientists, happens when a state turns its legitimate forms of power and violence against its own people. State violence is a breach of that social contract I described in the previous paragraph. Instead of a government using force to protect the population, state violence happens when the government uses force to control or harm the population. Governments can use violence, and even the *threat* of violence, to control, suppress, intimidate, or oppress its own people. That's what happened in Tiananmen Square, and that's what happened in Selma on the Edmund Pettus Bridge: the state was aiming its violence at its own citizens in an attempt to control them and make them stop expressing their frustrations with their government.

But there's another aspect of state violence that we need to consider. So far I have been talking about the relationship between a country and its own people, between a state and the citizens who make up that same nation. In some systems, though, not all of the people living within a country or under a government are citizens, and part of the power of government is the use of state violence to control or suppress people who have been conquered and whose land has been occupied. That was the case in the Judea described by the Book of Acts in the first century, when the Roman Empire controlled and governed the territory but when most of the people who lived there were not Roman citizens. And it has been the case in many places around the world, when some external power tries to control people using violence. In the modern world, we might think of Israel's use of violence against Palestinians as a good example; although they live in the same area and under the control of the same government as other Israelis, many Palestinians have fewer rights, less freedom, and far more exposure to state violence than do non-Palestinian Israelis. Or we could think about a place like Ukraine, where some Ukrainians live with the authority and violence of an occupying Russian force and are subject to a violent state that is not accountable to them, the people experiencing the violence itself.

People who study colonial systems often point out how violence helps establish and maintain uneven power relations. Earlier in this book I pointed out that in imperial or colonial systems, resources are drawn from the periphery to the center so that the centers of empires grow wealthy while the peripheries become stripped of resources. But violence flows in the opposite direction. In an empire or in a colonial system, violence is exported to the peripheries as a means of controlling and guaranteeing the extraction of wealth. The centers of empires, by contrast, tend to stay peaceful and safe. One of my favorite postcolonial political theorists, Achille Mbembe, has a particularly helpful way of putting this. "Civil peace in the West thus depends in large part on inflicting violence far away," Mbembe writes, "on lighting up centers of atrocities, and on the fiefdom wars and other massacres that accompany the establishment of strongholds and trading posts around the four corners of the planet."[1] Here, Mbembe is thinking mostly of European colonialism in Africa, Asia, and the Americas, where colonial powers used brutal violence against their subjects to suppress revolts and keep the people in line.

Although Mbembe and other people who study colonialism are usually thinking about the modern world, similar conditions pertained in Judea in the first century. Judea was a Roman province, having been conquered a few generations earlier by the Romans. As I mentioned previously, Judea was useful to Rome as a buffer against the Parthian Empire to the east and as a source for agricultural products and tax revenues. It was important to Rome to keep the people of Judea (and its other peripheral provinces and conquered peoples) in line and pacified. An imperial system depends on the exchange of violence for wealth, which is why the pages of the New Testament are filled with evidence of Roman domination. That's why Jesus ended up on a Roman cross—because the empire needed to exert control at every moment and squash any whisper of resistance or rebellion. And that's why the Book of Acts brings its story into so many points of contact with Roman power—because Rome maintained an infrastructure of violence from one end of its empire to the other. Acts describes a world dominated by state violence. The kind of imperial or colonial state violence found in Acts is not *quite* the same kind that was on display in

[1] Achille Mbembe, *Necropolitics*, trans. Steven Corcoran (Duke University Press, 2019), 19.

Tiananmen Square or at Kent State or on the Edmund Pettus Bridge. But the two forms of state violence are comparable and related to each other, and the story of violence in Acts will be useful to anyone living under the threat of state violence today.

State Violence in the Book of Acts

The first thing to say about violence in the Book of Acts is that the whole story Luke tells is bookended by implied state violence. Although Acts does not narrate either Jesus' death or Paul's death, those two deaths—at the hands of the Roman Empire—frame the entire narrative. Acts begins in the aftermath of Jesus' death on a Roman cross, and it ends with Paul in Roman custody in the capital city of Rome. At the beginning of Acts, Luke catches up the reader on the events of Jesus' life using strangely passive language. Instead of talking about Jesus' death by imperial execution, in Acts 1:2–3 Luke refers to "the day when he was taken up to heaven" and his appearances to the apostles "after his suffering." Luke almost goes out of his way to avoid mentioning imperial violence, to avoid asking the reader to look directly at it. And we have already discussed how, at the end of the book, Luke avoids saying much about what happened to Paul in Rome. It's possible that Luke simply did not know Paul's fate, but that explanation isn't very convincing, given the late date at which many scholars believe Acts was written. By the time Luke wrote Acts, the details of Paul's death probably would have been known. So Luke is playing it a bit coy with the details of state violence.

But in another sense, the whole narrative of Acts takes place against the backdrop of state violence. That's because of the timeline of Jesus' ministry and death, the events described in Acts, and the composition of Acts as it relates to the history of violence in the region. Speaking very roughly, Jesus' life probably stretched for the first three decades of the first century, and he likely died in the very early 30s. Acts describes events that took place between Jesus' death and roughly the late 50s to around the year 60, though it's hard to be precise. Recall that scholars don't agree on when the Book of Acts was written, though most of the options fall between about the years 70 and 115, and particularly about 80 to 90 C.E. But something very important and consequential happened between the events Acts describes and when they were written down, something I mentioned in the introduction of this book. Between 66 and 70, the province of Judea mounted an ill-fated and cataclysmic rebellion against Rome.

Luke never mentions the Jewish War in the Book of Acts, but it's always in the background of the narrative. As one of my favorite scholars, Paula Fredriksen, says about the time when Acts was being written, "the flames of Jerusalem in the year 70 backlight" the way Luke tells his story.[2] The Jewish War is never in the foreground of Acts, but it's always there in the background, illuminating everything else, because all the mainstream dates for the composition of Acts put the book after the conclusion of the war. The war couldn't help but affect the way Luke told the story of the decades leading up to the war's outbreak. In hindsight, as Luke was writing the story after the fact, the violence and destruction of the Jewish War shed a lot of light on everything that came before it. The Jewish War is a classic example of state violence used against non-citizen subjects. The Roman Empire depended on Judea for part of its security and revenue, so it was willing to inflict terrible violence on the province to keep it in line, just as Mbembe and other postcolonial theorists describe. Luke told the story of Acts knowing the Jewish War would break out eventually and knowing that the violence of the war would exact heavy costs on the peoples and the lands about which he was writing.

One way Luke foreshadowed the Jewish War was by telling Acts' story through the presence of various Roman officials, highlighting the ways Rome was a constant presence in the lives of Jesus' followers and in Judea leading up to the outbreak of the rebellion. Already we have met figures like Claudius Lysias, Felix, Porcius Festus, Agrippa and Bernice, Herod, the magistrates in Philippi, and various councils and officials elsewhere.

One person we have not yet met is a man named Cornelius, whose story Luke tells in Acts 10. He describes Cornelius as "a centurion of the Italian Cohort" (10:1) who was living in Caesarea—the same city where Paul would be held while Felix tried to squeeze a bribe from him. But the story of Cornelius involves not Paul but a different apostle—Peter. Through a vision, Cornelius heard God telling him to send for Peter, and meanwhile Peter received his own vision just before emissaries arrived from Cornelius to summon him.

The story of the interaction between Cornelius and Peter became a turning point in the debate among early Jesus followers about whether Jews and gentiles could share table fellowship and whether the burgeoning Jesus Movement would be friendly to gentiles at all. But instead of focusing on that aspect of the story here, I want to think about Cornelius as a way for Luke to gesture toward state violence—a way to foreshadow the violence of the Roman Empire and use it to cast light on the rest of the narrative.

Part of the tension behind the question of the relationship between Jews and gentiles would have been the complicated facts surrounding their interactions: many of the gentiles in Judea at the time would have been

[2] Paula Fredriksen, *When Christians Were Jews: The First Generation* (Yale University Press, 2018), 127.

representatives of Roman power. Rome had sent them there to settle, pacify, and subdue Judea and Judeans. So the question of Jews and gentiles sharing things in common was not simply one of ethnic or religious difference, but also of breaking bread with oppressors and occupiers. Although Acts tells the story of the interactions between Cornelius and Peter as one of religious purity, Luke makes sure to embed references to Roman power in the story. In 10:1 we learn that Cornelius was an important officer in the Roman military, and in 10:7 we find a reference to "a devout soldier from the ranks of those who served" Cornelius. There isn't external evidence for the Italian Cohort being stationed in Judea during this period (it was sent to Syria in the year 69, near the end of the Jewish War), so we don't know exactly what the cohort and the centurion were doing in Caesarea. But Caesarea, as we saw in the previous chapter, was the Roman administrative center in the region, so Cornelius was likely there as a key part of Rome's domination of Judea, as one of the people charged with unleashing violence to keep the people in line. Luke was telling this story on the other side of the Jewish War, knowing that Roman state violence had visited terrible destruction on Judea and immense loss of life on its people. He could have told Cornelius' story without identifying him as part of the Roman military occupation, but he chose to include that detail and to identify the men who worked under Cornelius as among the forces sent to keep Judea in line. Luke was reminding the readers of Acts that Roman violence was never very far out of sight.

A couple of chapters later, in 12:1–5, Luke includes another reminder for Acts' readers. Again, the reference is brief and curiously indirect, in a way reminiscent of how Luke dealt with the deaths of Jesus and Paul. "About that time King Herod laid violent hands upon some who belonged to the church," this passage says, and "he had James, the brother of John, killed with the sword." This would have been Herod Agrippa the First, the father of Agrippa and Bernice whom we met in the last chapter, and the grandson of Herod the Great, the king who had been on the throne at the time of Jesus' birth. The kings of the Herodian dynasty were clients of Rome propped up by the empire, used by Rome to keep order in Judea and the broader region. You could think of the arrangement as a way to outsource state violence: the Romans empowered the Herodians to suppress rebellion and dissent on their behalf. The Herodians got power out of the arrangement, and the Romans got to save some of their resources and keep their hands clean.

We are meant to understand Herod Agrippa's violent suppression of the Jesus Movement in that context: an example of local representatives of Roman power inflicting state violence on behalf of the empire. It's not clear what James and others in the Jesus Movement did to garner Herod's attention, but Herod likely was interested in cracking down on anything that caused unrest or built solidarity among the people. We should never underestimate the appeal of using state violence to build a leader's popularity. That seems to have been a big part of Herod's motivation; in 12:3, Acts tells us that when the killing of James proved popular with the people, "he proceeded to arrest Peter also." Then "when he had seized him, he put him in prison and handed him over to four squads of soldiers to guard him, intending to bring him out to the people after the Passover."

One interesting aspect of this episode is that Acts reports that James' death "pleased the Jews." Rather than emphasizing the way specific factions of Jews (or Judeans) like temple officials or Pharisees opposed the Jesus Movement, as had been the case so far in Acts, chapter 12 says that "the Jews" *as a whole* approved of James' death and inspired Herod to arrest Peter. Herod, then, seemed to be deploying state violence to play the middle between the Roman Empire and the Judean people; he was trying to manage his own position as Rome's representative by using the violence of the state selectively.

Some modern-day Christians read this comment about "the Jews" approving of James' death as evidence of Jewish disapproval of Christianity generally or of Jewish-Christian relations, but it's best to view this passage in light of the ways autocratic systems use violence to manipulate people. Violence, when inflicted or promised against one's enemies, is a seductive force. Many people want to see their opponents suffer or at least be taken down a peg. State violence, then, can be used to incentivize allegiance to the leader or to the state as a kind of payoff or bribe to one group of people at the expense of another. More on that in this chapter's final section.

By Acts 13:16–41, the scene has shifted away from James and Peter in Caesarea and Judea and toward Paul and Barnabas as they travel through Asia Minor. In a city called Antioch of Pisidia (to distinguish it from other Antiochs, namely the one in Syria), the apostles were visiting a synagogue on the sabbath, and the leaders asked Paul to say a few words. In his message to the synagogue, Paul focused on the history of Israel and argued that Israel's past had led inexorably to the present day and to the importance of Jesus. As part of his speech, Paul emphasized the role of state violence in the death of Jesus and especially the role of Pontius Pilate, who was governor at the time of Jesus' death. By emphasizing the Davidic lineage of Jesus, Paul's speech reminded the Jewish audience of their people's sovereignty and power. And by including the reference to Pilate, Paul reminded them it was Roman state violence that killed him.

In passages like this one, and in references to Roman power scattered throughout the book, Acts reminds its readers again and again of the role of Roman violence in their lives. The readers, living on the other side of the immense devastation of the Jewish War, would have read Luke's references to Roman officials—and their roles in the deaths of James and Jesus and the imprisonments of Peter, Paul, and others—as a foreshadowing. By describing figures like Cornelius and others in terms of their connections to Roman military power, Luke was building a world for his readers in which it would be impossible to forget that the Roman Empire had conquered Judea and was administering it as a Roman province by means of violence. Though Luke always stopped short of any outright critique of Rome, he also kept Rome front of mind as he told the story, never letting the empire off the hook for the ways its violence haunted the lives of the apostles.

Living with State Violence

Beginning in June of 2025, President Trump deployed the National Guard and other members of the military to several American cities. The first deployment was to Los Angeles. Trump's rationale: a "migrant invasion." Though state and local officials insisted there was no invasion or crisis, and though Los Angeles residents as a whole had sounded no alarm, Trump sent several thousand troops to the city. Many news reports connected the deployments to protests in Los Angeles only a few days earlier, in which citizens objected to the operations of ICE in the state and to Trump's programs of mass deportation. The deployed troops allegedly were supposed to aid local police in regaining control of a chaotic city, but local police insisted they did not need help, and news reports showed that the protests mostly stayed peaceful.

A couple of months later in August 2025, Trump deployed about two thousand National Guard troops to Washington, D.C., and federalized the D.C. police department. Trump called D.C. a "situation of complete and total lawlessness,"[3] though again local authorities neither asked for nor approved of the troops' presence in the city. By this time the deployments were being challenged successfully in courts, but Trump announced plans for further deployment of troops in cities like Memphis (with the approval of some state officials), Chicago (over the objections of local and state officials), and New Orleans. Alongside those deployments, ICE operations surged in some cities, including Charlotte and Minneapolis. In Minneapolis, the ICE surge resulted in weeks of disruptions to school and daily life, fear and terror, and (as of this writing) the murder of two people: Renée Good and Alex Pretti. Critics note

---

[3] Ana Faguy, "Trump Deploys National Guard to Washington DC and Pledges Crime Crackdown," *BBC News*, August 12, 2025, https://www.bbc.com/news/articles/cm2110me5g4o.

that the deployments and ICE targeting have focused on cities and states run by Democrats and that their populations tend to be composed of a majority or to include a substantial minority of non-White people.

These federal actions, carried out in cities controlled by the opposition party and populated by minorities, Trump justified in the name of safety and security. However, no real safety or security risks existed; in most cases, crime rates in those cities were already at historic lows. In an article about authoritarianism and misinformation, George Packer argues that authoritarian regimes thrive on polarizing the electorate into us and them [and that] authoritarian regimes and their allies flood the internet and social media with such a tide of falsehoods, so much uncertainty about what is true, so much distrust in traditional sources of information, that the public throws up its hands and checks out.

Regarding some of the federal actions I've just been discussing, and the ICE raids in particular, Packer says of Trump that "he sends masked police to pick people off the streets without probable cause for arrest, disappear them into secret prisons, and ship them off to random countries."[4] Trump wields the threat of state violence over people as well by deploying military units to cities as a display of force when there is no threat that warrants it. An action like deploying the National Guard to Los Angeles or Washington, D.C., is a threat against the people who live there, who are not generally the president's supporters. But it is also a kind of bribe or payoff to the people who *do* support the president, in the same way that Herod Agrippa's arrest of Peter was a way of rewarding loyalists with a display of state violence against their enemies.

The right response to state violence is to resist it, and that resistance can look like peaceful protests, action in the courts, and an insistence that the military obey only lawful orders (as several prominent lawmakers have recently done, including Sen. Mark Kelly, who faced backlash from administration officials). And the right response to the misinformation and polarization that justify that violence is to seek out reliable forms of information and resist falsehoods. These responses might feel feeble in the face of military strength. The lesson of the Book of Acts is that state violence often does inflict incalculable damage and that an autocrat who wants to hurt people often will be able to do so. But the lesson learned from the man standing in front of a line of tanks in Tiananmen Square, blocking their progress, is that resistance is powerful, even if it is symbolic resistance, and even if the fruits of resistance are not always visible in the moment.

---

[4] George Packer, "America's Zombie Democracy," *The Atlantic*, September 24, 2025, https://www.theatlantic.com/ideas/archive/2025/09/america-authoritarian-regime-ai-suicide/684350/.

Further Reading

Early in this chapter I mentioned and quoted the work of Achille Mbembe, who is among my favorite theorists of colonial systems and postcolonial cultures. His work *Necropolitics* will be interesting to anyone who thinks about the ways governments enforce power and deploy the military against everyday people.[5] Mbembe's work, in turn, relies heavily on the writings of Frantz Fanon, an intellectual who wrote extensively about French colonialism in the Caribbean and North Africa. His books *The Wretched of the Earth*[6] and *Black Skin, White Masks*[7] are both fiery and incisive reports into the inner workings of colonialism, and neither shies away from the role of state violence in controlling and pacifying territory. I also enjoy the writings of Judith Butler, who is best known for work on gender theory but who also has written extensively on power and violence. Butler's book *Frames of War* helps us to think about the variety of ways lives and bodies are treated and conceived in the rhetoric and practice of violence.[8]

---

[5] Achille Mbembe, *Necropolitics*.

[6] Frantz Fanon, *The Wretched of the Earth*, trans. Richard Philcox (Grove Press, 2004).

[7] Frantz Fanon, *Black Skin, White Masks* (Grove Press, 2008).

[8] Judith Butler, *Frames of War: When Is Life Grievable?* (Verso, 2016).

8

Protecting Money

While I was in divinity school, I joined a school trip to Cuernavaca, Mexico. As part of the trip we spent about ten days learning about the history and culture of the area and the people who lived there—the Nahuatl-speaking cultures that had flourished in the area prior to European conquest, the period of colonization and the introduction of Christianity to the region, and especially the modern period. Our visit took place only about a decade after the implementation of NAFTA, or the North American Free Trade Agreement, a huge treaty between the United States, Mexico, and Canada that encouraged trade among the three nations by lowering tariffs and other barriers. The trade agreement had been controversial in the United States, leading to fears that manufacturing jobs would be lost to Mexico and leading to political backlash when that turned out to be true. I was already familiar with NAFTA from the American perspective, since it had been a big matter of national debate since I was a kid. But I was not prepared for the way the treaty had changed life in Mexico.

Cuernavaca is a sizeable city not far from Mexico City, a long way from the border with the United States. Because it was so far from the border, I had not anticipated that the city would have been affected by the change in trade policies. In my naïve imagination, it was only the cities along the border whose economies would be significantly transformed. But upon our arrival in Cuernavaca, we were greeted by a cityscape in transition. Large parts of the city were transforming into industrial zones, with huge multinational corporations building enormous factories surrounded by tall chain-link fences topped with barbed wire. Some of the factories looked like prisons with watchtowers overlooking the surrounding area. Corporate emblems adorned the stark white walls of the factories, announcing the presence of the chemical firms and automobile manufacturers that had quickly built facilities in Mexico to take advantage of NAFTA's new provisions. They were there to pay low wages to Mexican workers to build products that would be shipped north to Canada and the United States, where wealthier consumers would buy the products and ensure nice profits for the corporations.

As we talked with the local people, we learned more about how NAFTA had affected life in the city and across Mexico. Suddenly work was easier to find, as the factories ramped up production for export to the United States and Canada to take advantage of Mexico's cheap labor. People in the surrounding region abandoned traditional farming and time-tested forms of self-sufficiency to chase the allure of factory wages. Rural folks migrated to the city, disrupting family systems in the process. And in certain parts of town, as the corporations bought up land for their factories, they sometimes displaced longtime residents and short-term squatters.

Our group spoke with members of a small Catholic community struggling to adapt to the new economy—mostly very poor people who had traded their support systems in a village for the promise of a factory job in the city. We met the members of that community in a one-room church building in the kind of shabby makeshift neighborhood the factory workers could afford, and I remember singing a hymn with them that translates into English as "It's Not Enough to Pray." The hymn represented the community's conviction that, while they found comfort in religion, they felt that their government and the international community had abandoned them. For them, prayers were helpful but not enough.

A couple of days after we met with those people, we also traveled to a mansion not far away, in a very nice part of town, a mansion ringed with a high fence and hedges and monitored by security guards. There, we talked poolside with the owner of an auto parts supplier, who had grown wealthy thanks to NAFTA by making parts for the new car manufacturing plants in town and exporting the parts north to the United States and Canada for use in plants there.

At first the man was friendly and gracious as we sat on his patio, and he seemed pleased to play host to a group of American students. But soon he became angry with us as we peppered him with questions about the ethics of what he was doing. From his perspective, he was providing jobs to people who had not had jobs before. And he was right. But we were learning to see how the effects of capitalism extended well beyond the job of an employee or the profits of an employer. We were learning to see how a factory in Cuernavaca not only mattered for the land and the people of that place, but also how it was connected to and affected the land and people elsewhere. Money's tendrils stretch wide and deep.

What surprised me most about my time in Cuernavaca were the security forces and police that surrounded many of the factories and patrolled the roads that led to them. Men in uniform not only eyed us suspiciously as we slowed down to gawk at the giant boxy metal shells of the growing factories, but they also descended on us quickly to tell us we needed to keep moving. The police and security guards were on edge, as if they expected threats from every direction. They didn't want us taking photographs.

Meanwhile, in the parts of town where there were no new factories, police were scarce. Those we did see lolled on street corners or sat listlessly in their cars. As long as the pedestrians and motorbikes kept moving, the police seemed content.

But the police and the guards near the factories were almost aggressively vigilant in the attention they paid to everything around them. Behind them, company logos gleamed on the sides of the factory walls, reminding everyone whose interests the police and guards were there to protect.

Protecting Money

Like clockwork, a few days into any major crisis or disaster in an American city, there are news stories about looting. It happened in New Orleans in the wake of Hurricane Katrina as desperate people scavenged for any food or medical supplies they could find. Breathless news anchors ran stories about lawless looting. It happened in Los Angeles during the riots that followed the acquittal of four officers who had been charged with excessive force in the beating of Rodney King, and scenes of burning convenience stores quickly overshadowed King's story. In Minneapolis following the murder of George Floyd in police detention, and in Ferguson after police shot Michael Brown, news stories about looting soon crowded out coverage of the police violence itself. In the aftermath of fires, hurricanes, and mass protests, there is almost always a story about looting, even if the looting isn't the real story at all.

Of course, looting sometimes happens, and it is costly to the businesses and communities where it occurs. In the frustration, fraying of norms, and sometimes desperate need that accompanies those moments, people break into businesses to steal and vandalize. But many observers have noticed how quickly stories about looting displace stories about the tragedy itself. Media depictions of Hurricane Katrina's devastation of New Orleans' poorest neighborhoods quickly became a sideshow to sensationalized and sometimes wholly fabricated stories about looters damaging and stealing property. There seems to be something about looting that TV cameras can't resist—something the urgent voices of cable news anchors cannot leave alone. In those moments it becomes clear how deeply we are concerned for property and how quickly we forget our concern for *people* and instead wring our hands about *stuff*.

People from cultures that value community over individuals—cultures that are not steeped in European principles of property ownership and supercharged American versions of capitalism—often will point out how strange the American fixation on property really is. Having grown up in the United States and imbibed the values of capitalism from a young age, I've had to work to understand their viewpoint. They are right: we Americans tend to fetishize individual property, and we impose harsh penalties on people who steal or damage it. Sometimes it seems as if our concern for people pales in comparison. Recall the case of David Coulson, who was sentenced to life in prison in California for stealing fourteen dollars from an unlocked garage. After decades in prison, Coulson was recently released after a judge reviewed his case and determined that the punishment far exceeded the crime.[1] Or take the example of Fair Wayne Bryant, a Louisiana man who stole a pair of hedge clippers. Bryant likewise was sentenced to life in prison.[2] Many factors go into these kinds of sentences, including laws designed to escalate penalties steeply for repeat offenders. But the logic of capitalism also bears much of the blame. A society that privileges property and wealth tends to respond severely to any attack on physical things and money. Like in Cuernavaca, where the big multinational corporations were building their factories, whenever money moves in we develop strict security systems meant to keep that money safe. And if someone takes money (or whatever it represents), as in the cases of Coulton and Bryant, the penalties are often disproportionately harsh. This is not solely a modern American problem or even a multinational capitalism problem. Acts narrates the same patterns two thousand years ago, describing swift and harsh responses to threats to money and property.

Protecting Money in Acts

The Book of Acts contains several interesting stories about money. For instance, near the beginning of the book we read about a married couple, Ananias and Sapphira, who deceive their community of believers by mutually and secretly agreeing to withhold a portion of the proceeds from selling some property. Shortly afterward, both of them are dead. Acts does not say precisely *why* they died, but both suddenly expire, one after the other, their scheme having been discovered. Maybe they died of shock and shame, or maybe God killed them; Acts is coy about the exact cause of death but makes clear that hoarding money is deadly. (I'll have more to say about this story in the next chapter.)

Another interesting story about money comes closer to the end of Acts, in chapter 19. There, Acts mentions stories about Paul's miraculous deeds of healing side by side with the story of "some itinerant Jewish exorcists" who were also engaged in healing work, and Acts gives special attention to the "seven sons of a Jewish high priest named Sceva" (19:13–14), who seemed to be profiting

---

[1] Sam Levin, "Sentenced to Life for Stealing $14: 'I Needed Help, But Was Given Jail,'" *The Guardian*, November 2, 2022, https://www.theguardian.com/us-news/2022/nov/02/sentenced-to-life-for-stealing-14-i-needed-help-but-was-given-jail.

[2] Alanah Odoms Hebert, "The Law That Sent a Man to Prison for Life for Stealing a Pair of Hedge Clippers—and What Prosecutors Can Do About It," American Civil Liberties Union, October 2, 2020, https://www.aclu.org/news/criminal-law-reform/the-law-that-sent-a-man-to-prison-for-life-for-stealing-a-pair-of-hedge-clippers-and-what-prosecutors-can-do-about-it.

from their work as faith-healing exorcists and magicians. (Sceva is otherwise unknown in the historical record. His name is not a Jewish name, and it does not make sense that a Jewish high priest would be located in Ephesus where this part of the story takes place. For those reasons, many scholars consider this story to be unhistorical.) Sceva and his seven sons are revealed as phonies when one of the spirits they are attempting to exorcise calls them on their fraud and assaults them, and in response "a number of those who practiced magic collected their books and burned them publicly," presumably to avoid being beaten up by evil spirits, and "when the value of these books was calculated, it was found to come to fifty thousand silver coins" (19:19).

As interesting as those two stories about money are, I want to focus on two other stories from Acts to demonstrate the way greed for material wealth came into conflict with the protagonists of the book. We have already seen these stories in other contexts, as they both represent themes of earlier chapters like violence, imprisonment, and the repurposing of history for nationalist agendas. But here I want to think about these two stories—the story of Paul casting out the spirit of divination from the enslaved girl in Philippi and the story of the silversmiths inciting a riot in Ephesus—as evidence of how money and property drive people's behaviors and commitments and how the actions and proclamations of Paul and his companions felt threatening to people who owned property.

We have already encountered the story of Paul casting the spirit of divination out from the enslaved girl in Acts 16:16–40, and I have already said a few things about the strangeness and unfairness of the story. The strangeness comes from the fact that, at least as Acts tells the story, the enslaved girl with the spirit of divination was only telling the truth about Paul and his companions. "These men are slaves of the Most High God, who proclaim to you a way of salvation" (16:17), the girl shouted to them as they went about their business. That was a claim with which Paul and his colleagues undoubtedly would have agreed, and perhaps it was even precisely the way they would have described themselves. But the girl's proclamations continued "for many days," and Paul became "very much annoyed," as Acts says in 16:18. Out of his annoyance, and perhaps frustrated by her repeated shouting in his direction, Paul ordered the spirit of divination to come out of her.

In chapter 2 of this book I mentioned that the translation "spirit of divination" used by the NRSVue and some other modern translations is a simplification of a more complex Greek phrase that literally means something like "a spirit of the python," and this strange label probably referred to the girl's association with cultic activities at a religious center called Delphi. Delphi was famous across the ancient Mediterranean world as a cultic site and the home of a famous oracle from whom people could receive pronouncements about their fates and futures. So the "spirit of divination" that the girl possessed (or that possessed her) might have been a kind of prophetic gift, the ability to see the future or to fortune-tell. That's why modern editions of Acts in English translate the phrase as "a spirit of divination." If it was true that the girl was associated with Delphi and its prophetic activities, it would account for the precision with which the girl was able to read Paul and Silas and their companions and to give an accurate account of their purpose. Paul did not turn on the girl because she was wrong or because the spirit possessing her was malevolent. From what Acts tells us, the enslaved girl was only speaking the truth. Instead, Paul turned on her because he found her annoying.

The way this story is told in Acts does not demonstrate much concern for the girl herself, as I discussed in chapter 2. Stripped of her prophetic gift, the enslaved girl suddenly became far less valuable economically, and that devaluation likely led to a steep decline in her standards of living and an increase in the kinds of violence and abuse to which she was exposed. An enslaved person with a special skill or ability, even while still enslaved, could demand better treatment and respect. But without her prophetic gift, the girl's status would have plummeted, and her life likely became far more miserable.

After Paul drove the spirit of divination from her, though, the Book of Acts did not continue to follow the story of the enslaved girl. Instead, in a way that is not so different from the patterns of TV news channels after a tragedy, Acts paid attention to the money. "But when her owners saw that their hope of making money was gone," Acts tells us, "they seized Paul and Silas and dragged them into the marketplace before the authorities" (16:19). The Greek word for "marketplace" here is *agora*, which was a public space in the center of most cities. The *agora* was in fact a marketplace, but it was also much more than that: it was a public forum, the location of courts where officials kept office hours, and an administrative center. A city's *agora* was its heart—the place where the city's spirit lived. It makes sense that the girl's owners took the apostles there, where local officials were waiting and going about their business. But their destination in the marketplace was also symbolic of the ways the grievances of the enslaved girl's owners were rooted in both civic and financial concerns—or money and pride.

Although Luke tells us that the enslaved girl's owners were worried about their ability to profit from her prophetic gift, the owners told a different story to the city magistrates. "These men, are disturbing our city," they said in 16:20–21. "These men, these Jews, are disturbing our city," they said in 16:20-21, "and are advocating customs that are not lawful for us, being Romans, to adopt or observe." As we saw in chapter 2, the city's magistrates moved quickly to have the apostles stripped and beaten and thrown into jail, "in the innermost cell and fastened their feet in the stocks" (16:24). The enslaved girl's owners framed their personal, economic grievances in terms of civic, almost patriotic concerns. While Paul and Silas had really injured only them (and the enslaved girl most of all), not the whole town, and while the damage to the owners was financial in nature, the owners framed their complaint in terms of custom, law, and civic disturbance. They transformed their personal grievances into grounds upon which the whole society ought to be concerned, and they magnified an interpersonal dispute into a symbolic clash of ideals. Their way of describing Paul and Silas, "these men, these Jews," drew attention to the ethnicity of the apostles and emphasized their foreignness. It was a way for them to make sure everyone understood their trouble with Paul and Silas as an us-versus-them kind of thing. The enslaved girl's owners were making sure that the magistrates and everyone else understood the conflict in terms of insiders and outsiders, locals and interlopers, good guys and bad guys.

This is often how it goes when money is concerned. From the perspective of the enslaved girl's owners, they have experienced damage to their capital. Although today we would reject the idea that a person like the enslaved girl was an asset, a piece of property, or a means of production, by the logic of the time that was what she was—she was a possession used to make money. By casting out the spirit of divination from the girl and making her unfit for that purpose, Paul committed a sin against the markets and against property, and he unwittingly triggered the kind of response that an attack on capital often provokes. Paul and Silas only received a beating and a half a night in jail before a divinely sent earthquake set them free. But if God had not been there to throw open the prison doors, they might have met a fate like those of David Coulson or Fair Wayne Bryant—the men ordered to serve life in prison for petty theft. They might have found that even small acts that damage capital and wealth often will be met by intense and heavy-handed punishment.

The other major story in Acts about protecting money—the story of the silversmiths' riot in Ephesus—has some themes in common with the story of the enslaved girl in Philippi. In Ephesus as in Philippi, the issue was that property and wealth were threatened; and in Ephesus as in Philippi, the dispute was dressed up in terms of civic pride. In some ways, though, this story in Ephesus is a little less like the stories of the men who were locked away for stealing negligible amounts of wealth and more like the story in Cuernavaca, where corporations erected tall fences around their investments and patrolled the boundaries around them to make sure everyone knew to keep away. In Cuernavaca the fences were real and the guards were watching from their SUVs. But in Ephesus the silversmiths patrolled the perimeter of their business just as vigilantly using civic pride and mob violence.

In chapter 2 I told this story about Ephesus as a story about nationalism, as a case of "Make Ephesus Great Again." That's how Demetrius, the silversmith who was leading the case against Paul, described the stakes of the conflict. "Men, you know that we get our wealth from this business," Demetrius began in 19:25, speaking to his fellow silversmiths. "You also see and hear that not only in Ephesus but in almost the whole of Asia this Paul has persuaded and drawn away a considerable number of people by saying that gods made with hands are not gods" (19:26). Here, Demetrius made the economic case, focusing on the potential damage to their business, which draws its clientele from all of Asia Minor, what is now the country of Turkey. But then Demetrius shifted his argument. "And there is danger," he continued, "not only that this trade of ours may come into disrepute but also that the temple of the great goddess Artemis will be scorned, and she will be deprived of her majesty that brought all Asia and the world to worship her" (19:27). That patriotic argument did the trick. The men began to shout in rage, "Great is Artemis of the Ephesians!" (19:28), and a riot began.

The ease with which Demetrius started by attacking Paul as a threat to the private finances of artisans in a specific industry, then shifted to describing Paul's actions as an attack on a whole city and people and a venerable goddess, was impressive. Even when speaking only to the silversmiths themselves, Demetrius began with a nod to their collective livelihood then quickly pivoted to a much broader appeal to civic pride and religious devotion. Perhaps he knew that it is hard to get someone to riot because of a decrease in another person's income and that it is easier to appeal to religious or political allegiances to get people on your side. It worked. It didn't take long for the silversmiths' concerns to balloon and involve a much bigger segment of the city. A couple of interesting details in 19:31–32 show the scale of the uprising. In 19:31, even some provincial officials seemed to be aware that the silversmiths had incited a mob and had gathered in the city's theater, and they warned Paul through back channels not to go to the theater. That suggests that the disturbance was affecting the whole city and was becoming known even beyond Ephesus. And in 19:32, Luke tells us that the gathering was so large and chaotic that most of the people in the theater had no clue why they had gathered in the first place; they had simply joined the crowd as it rushed into the theater, following the angry energy as it bubbled over.

That is sometimes how it goes with property and wealth. A mob mentality takes over, and reason and proportion go out the window. As long as Donald Trump has been a fixture of national politics, he has held broadly anti-immigrant positions, including many repeated claims that immigrants are criminals and even animals. But during the 2024 presidential campaign, Trump began to use an economic argument more frequently, and he framed it in terms of economic solidarity in the same way the Ephesian silversmiths did. According to the Marshall Project, Trump claimed at least 155 times that immigrants (especially migrants from Mexico) were "taking our jobs."[3] In that 2024 campaign, when Trump was trying to win the support of Black and Latino voters specifically, he often described an immigrant threat to what he sometimes called "Black jobs" and "Hispanic jobs." On August 26 of that year, for example, Trump said that "African American families, Hispanic American families, their jobs are being taken. Unrelated to you, but their jobs are being taken." A few days later, Trump claimed that "they're coming in by [the] millions and millions, and a lot of them are taking the jobs for the Black population, the Hispanic population." And speaking of the Biden administration a few days earlier, Trump claimed that "because they lie so much, the jobs he created, almost all of them, almost 100%, people say more than 100%, went to illegal aliens." Leaving aside the question of how "more than 100%" of jobs could have gone to "illegal aliens," Trump's rhetorical strategy was clear during that stretch of August of 2024: to describe immigration as a threat to the economic security of Americans, but specifically to portray immigrants as a predatory population stealing the jobs of Black and Latino Americans. The comments sparked trends on social media in which people wondered what, exactly, a "Black job" or a "Hispanic job" is. But the strategy might have worked; in many places, Trump made marginal gains among Black voters and substantial gains among Latino voters.

Sometimes political observers talk about "economic anxiety" as a root cause for anti-immigrant sentiment, and Donald Trump is hardly the first politician to capitalize on that. Truthfully, though, economists have long pointed out that immigration is only one of many factors contributing to the economic stresses felt by Americans and that on balance immigrants help energize the economy rather than drain or slow it down. Some economists and journalists have even begun to ask how certain industries will find the labor to function if Trump's immigration strategy takes hold permanently.[4] From a strictly economic perspective, immigration is not the crisis Trump and other politicians say it is. But immigration remains a useful way to harness the energy created by "economic anxiety" because it can be easier to blame outsiders than to pay

---

[3] Rachel Dissell, "They've Taken the Jobs of African Americans and Hispanics, and That Was Obvious to Me. Next Is Gonna to Be Unions, You Watch," The Marshall Project, accessed July 10 2026, https://www.themarshallproject.org/2024/10/21/fact-check-12000-trump-statements-immigrants#taking_jobs_from_americans.

[4] Lydia DePillis and Campbell Robertson, "What America Might Look Like With Zero Immigration," *New York Times*, December 28, 2025, https://www.nytimes.com/2025/12/28/business/us-immigration-trump-1920s.html.

attention to the internal structures of a society with steep economic disparities and wealth discrepancies.

The silversmiths undoubtedly felt that it was hard to make a living. But it is unlikely it had much to do with a couple of out-of-town Judeans who had come preaching about some new religion. Instead, the silversmiths, like everyone else in Ephesus, were part of a sprawling empire in which everyone's labor and everyone's economic output served the purposes of a central ruling elite. Everything about their lives and business, from the mines where the silver was extracted to the roads the pilgrims used to travel to the temple of Artemis to the theater where they gathered to shout against Paul, was in the service of empire and the autocratic rulers who benefitted from it. The silversmiths could point all they wanted to foreigners like Paul as the culprit, but that wouldn't change anything. The system was always going to be tilted against them.

Living in a Society that Protects Money

In Cuernavaca, when we visited the small Catholic community that had sprung up there in the shadow of the new factories, the people had a lot to say about solidarity. Solidarity is a way of describing how people can rely on each other for support and build bonds with each other rather than seeing each other as enemies. I will have a lot more to say about solidarity in chapters 9 and 10, where we will focus on strategies for living under autocracies, authoritarian regimes, and empires. For now, though, I will point out that the people of that church community in Cuernavaca quickly decided they would be safer and more powerful together than apart and that they could not rely on the economic power of large corporations to protect them. The security guards and fences, they realized right away, were not there for the benefit of everyday people.

In Ephesus, when the Jews in the crowd pushed Alexander to the front and nominated him to take charge of the angry gathering in the theater, a glimmer of solidarity began to shine through. It wasn't much; there was hardly a revolution going on in the theater in that moment. But there was a recognition that, in Alexander's words, the blame had gone too far and that safety and security would not be found in blaming outsiders or concocting conspiracies about who might be damaging the silversmithing business. Instead, as Alexander spoke, he pointed out a few basic realities. First, in 19:35, Alexander reminded the people that despite the furor and anxiety, Ephesus retained its cultural renown and economic power (as the United States does today). Second, in 19:37, he pointed out that the people they had dragged into the theater were not actually responsible for the actions of which they had been accused. Third, Alexander recommended that people pursue their complaints through legitimate means.

And finally, in 19:40—and most effectively, I think—Alexander reminded the riled-up silversmiths and the other Ephesians that all of them, foreigner or not, were subject to the law of the Roman Empire, and that all of them were at that moment in danger of being charged with rioting. This last point from Alexander—that the empire retained its power over everyone—was a way of reframing the solidarity of the situation. Instead of seeing things as Ephesians versus foreigners or insiders versus outsiders, the more objectively truthful perspective was to understand that they were all subjects of the same empire and that all of them lived under the thumb of an immense military and economic power. The fears and anxieties they felt stemmed from that empire, not from each other.

The same is true for us. While politicians and autocratic leaders often try to divide us and convince us that we are all responsible for each other's problems, the truth is that American citizens and immigrants alike live within the same systems that exploit us all economically and protect money rather than people. The rhetoric of who is taking whose jobs is a distraction from the fact that wealth is increasingly concentrated in the hands of corporations and their rich owners and that the barbed-wire fences surrounding those corporations' factories ostensibly to protect us are actually there to protect money.

Further Reading

One of my favorite takes on the story of the enslaved girl in Philippi comes from Katy Valentine, who points out how the girl was treated is as an obstacle for Paul and as a literary device for Luke. It's a clever way to look under the surface of a story and see how the narrative is constructed with certain values and ends in mind.[5] As I mentioned earlier in this book, the work of Mitzi Smith,[6] Christy Cobb,[7] Katherine Shaner,[8] Jennifer Glancy,[9] and Candida Moss[10] shed much light on ancient practices of slavery and the ways they show up in the New Testament and in interpretations of it.

---

[5] Katy E. Valentine, "Reading the Slave Girl of Acts 16:16–18 in Light of Enslavement and Disability," *Biblical Interpretation* 26, no. 3 (2018): 352–68.

[6] Mitzi Smith, "Slavery and the Early Church," in *True to Our Native Land: An African American New Testament Commentary*, ed. Brian K. Blount et al. (Fortress Press, 2007).

[7] Christy Cobb, *Slavery, Gender, Truth, and Power in Luke-Acts and Other Ancient Narratives* (Palgrave Macmillan, 2019).

[8] Katherine A. Shaner, *Enslaved Leadership in Early Christianity* (Oxford University Press, 2018).

[9] Jennifer Glancy, *Slavery in Early Christianity* (Oxford University Press, 2002).

[10] Candida Moss, *God's Ghostwriters: Enslaved Christians and the Making of the Bible* (Little, Brown and Company, 2024).

PART III

Living under Autocracy

Part III of this book shifts attention to living under autocratic systems and the strategies that can produce thriving communities of flourishing and resistance. Chapter 9 considers community—the kinds of community described and envisioned in the Book of Acts and the kinds of community that help us thrive today. And chapter 10 thinks about togetherness and the practices of diversity, equity, and inclusion that characterized the Jesus Movement in Acts and that can help us to build just and healthy communities in our own place and time.

9

Community

A little stand of aspen trees lines the side yard of our house in Denver. The trees begin near the back fence, where I think the first ones must have been planted, as the trunks there are the thickest and tallest. As the stand stretches toward the front of the house, an aspen tree punches out of the ground every six or eight feet, its bark silver against the green leaves of the other shrubs. On the leading edge, closest to the street, the aspens are young, and their trunks are only the width of a thumb or a broom handle. New saplings pop up every spring, growing quickly, straight up to the sky. Each year the stand migrates a few feet toward the street; the oldest and largest ones on the trailing edge die off, and the new shoots pop out of the ground, hoping for the best.

The aspens can do that because though they look like individual trees, they are all part of a single organism. Aspens are clonal, meaning that they are connected at the roots, and every new individual tree is a copy of all the rest. In the wild, in good conditions, an individual tree might live for decades or even more than a century. But the root system—the clonal colony—persists long after any individual tree's life begins or ends, and the stand is always pushing up new trees to explore new territories. The most famous stand of aspens, an enormous and ancient colony in Utah called Pando, might have been growing for eighty thousand years, and for millennia it has been replacing its dying trunks with new springtime shoots.

Although all of the trunks in our garden now will be gone one day, the roots will still be connected underground, and they will still be sending up new shoots every spring.

At their best, human communities work that way too. In places like the United States, we have been taught to think like individuals and to pit ourselves against each other in search of money, prestige, honor, and safety. We are taught to think that any success I get must be taken from you, and any security you have must come at my expense. We have learned to prioritize self over the communal good and to think in terms of individual rights rather than of our obligations to one another. This is especially true in situations of scarcity; we have been conditioned to think of life as a zero-sum game, with winners and losers. When we find ourselves in autocratic systems like authoritarian regimes and empires—systems that emphasize loyalty to one leader, or to a small group of leaders, and that emphasize rewards for some and punishments for others—the problem becomes especially pronounced. We begin to think that everyone has to look out for themselves and that security and prosperity can be found only by hewing closely to the leaders' favor and ingratiating ourselves as much as possible. We seek our safety in success, but we forget the lesson of the aspens: that we flourish when we emphasize our connections and share our resources with each other.

The Strength of Community

As a form of government, autocracy can take several forms. Autocracies can be headed by a dictator, someone who has seized control of the apparatus of government and who rules with absolute power. Or an autocracy can concentrate power in the hands of one person by design, as in a monarchy, where a single ruler wields the power of the state by virtue of their position in a family.

The Roman Empire was somewhere between those two models, though by the time of the New Testament it was closer to a monarchy than a dictatorship. Decades before Jesus was born, a man named Octavian usurped much of the power that had traditionally belonged to the Senate and other parts of the Roman aristocracy. Octavian used the assassination of his adopted father, Julius Caesar, as a pretext for his power grab. Reigning under the name Augustus, he became the Caesar, the head of a Roman Empire that stretched thousands of miles, and ordered and ruled millions of people. His position was passed down over time, sometimes from father to son, sometimes in more complicated arrangements, and eventually, long after the period of the New Testament, even including several Caesars reigning at once. But in the time that the events described in the Book of Acts were taking place, and when the book itself was being written, the Roman Empire was well on its way to autocracy, with fewer and fewer checks on the power and authority of one person, the Caesar, the emperor.

Authoritarianism, by contrast, is a style of leadership or a way of ruling. Whereas autocracy is a *form* of government, authoritarianism is more like a *posture*—an approach or method to using the power of the state. Authoritarianism is a way to make autocracy work. Authoritarianism insists on the correctness of the ruler at all times, and it cannot tolerate criticism of the person who is in charge. Usually authoritarianism relies on force and violence, or at least the *threat* of force and violence, to achieve uniformity of opinion. Authoritarianism favors bullies and cares very little about debate, persuasion, or mutuality. With time, whatever other institutions belong to the government—like courts, congresses, and local legislatures—are subsumed under the power of the ruler or otherwise neutralized.

In the case of the Roman Empire, this happened both suddenly and all at once. Augustus and his successors often took steps to limit or neutralize the power of others in the government, and they reacted harshly against anyone who challenged their own authority.

A further complicating feature of the Roman Empire is that it was just that—an empire. The Romans governed themselves close to home, in the center of the Roman Empire, but they also governed subjects in territories spread across all ends of the Mediterranean basin, from North Africa to Britain and from Spain to Syria and Judea. In many of those places, they ruled using the domination of imperial violence, economic power, and propaganda. The violence of the empire was not evenly applied, but it landed more heavily on the people who were subjects but not citizens—the conquered peoples who made up a majority of the Roman Empire's population.

Both autocracy and authoritarianism are opposed to democracy. Historically, democracy has roots in several different cultures across multiple continents, and it has looked different in different places and times. Throughout its history, the United States has been a democracy of one form or another, even though for long periods of its history certain classes of people (women, enslaved persons, immigrants) were not allowed to participate. The hallmarks of democracy include the power of people themselves to decide on the laws that will govern them, either directly or by electing representatives. That feature—making such decisions by voting in elections—is a core aspect of democratic systems. In ancient Rome the population didn't get to vote for Caesar, and Caesar didn't always need to worry very much about the opinions of the people he ruled. But in a democratic system the people retain the right and authority to determine the terms of their own governance and sovereignty resides ultimately with the people themselves, not with any particular ruler.

I wanted to go through all of that in order to sketch some of the options that groups of people have for organizing themselves. Although I have mostly been talking about the ways states are organized and governed (especially the Roman Empire and the United States of America), versions of these models also pertain to other kinds of groups. If you think about the different models of church governance, for instance, you can see some of these options reflected in the most common models of polity. Likewise, professional organizations, social groups, and even families use aspects of these models to organize their lives. The models of governance a group chooses typically say a lot about the values that group holds. By the same token, the form of governance will help shape those values moving forward. A group that relies on the authority of a single person will organize its life around that person's desires, capabilities, and whims. But a group that relies on the community to govern itself through some form of democracy will reflect and cultivate the values of democratic systems.

Those values reflected and cultivated in democratic systems include things like equality, equity, participation, collectivism, and individual freedom. That is not to say every democratic system *achieves* those things. But those are the ideals toward which democratic ideals point, as opposed to authoritarian or autocratic systems, which privilege a unitary executive with lots of power, hierarchy, and limits on individual freedoms and which cater to the idiosyncratic anxieties and desires of the leader.

In the United States today, under the presidency of Donald Trump, many political scientists think the system is moving toward autocracy and that the government's tactics are becoming more authoritarian.[1] Congress has ceded to him many of its core responsibilities, like the power of the purse, war powers, tariff authority, and oversight of foreign affairs. The Supreme Court has repeatedly sided with the administration in precedent-shattering decisions, including offering the president substantial immunity for nearly any acts that can be construed as "official." Life in the United States under the presidency of Donald Trump has taken a hard turn toward autocracy and authoritarianism and away from democracy.

It can be difficult to know how to build and maintain community in a moment like this one; it can be tough to understand the best shape to offer to our life together. Fortunately, the Book of Acts includes stories of life under autocratic rule, and it suggests patterns of life that help us respond to moments of authoritarian control. As it turns out, those patterns are not so different from the ones used by aspen trees.

Community in the Book of Acts

The Book of Acts contains many stories of conflict and disagreement, plenty of times when fear and even violence ruled the day. But especially in the early chapters of Acts, the book also contains beautiful descriptions of communities at peace internally and at peace with the people around them.

[1] Andrew Marantz, "Is It Happening Here?," *The New Yorker*, April 28, 2025, https://www.newyorker.com/magazine/2025/05/05/is-the-us-becoming-an-autocracy.

Among the stories of riots, mobs, stonings, and angry accusations, Acts also tells us about how the members of the earliest Jesus Movement were constructing and living their lives together and how the followers of Jesus built community with intentionality.

We have already seen in earlier chapters of this book that the 30s and 40s of the first century—the era that the early chapters of Acts describe—were a tumultuous and fraught moment in time. The Jewish War was only a couple of decades away, and already Judea was a tinderbox of apocalyptic expectations, warring factions, and imperial domination. With the memories of Jesus' execution still fresh, and with Roman troops patrolling the streets of Jerusalem and the backroads of Judea, it would have made sense for Jesus' followers to retreat into isolation, guardedness, and fear.

Instead, Acts describes Jesus' first followers as living in something like a utopia. "All these were constantly devoting themselves to prayer," 1:14 says, "together with certain women, including Mary the mother of Jesus, as well as his brothers." Their unity went far beyond prayer. The apostles were living in a kind of intentional community of shared resources and mutual support. It was not a perfect community, but faced with the trauma of state violence and the fear that the Roman Empire instilled, the apostles clearly chose community over division. For a good example of what their community was like, take a look at Acts 2:42–47:

> They devoted themselves to the apostles' teaching and fellowship, to the breaking of bread and the prayers. Awe came upon everyone, because many wonders and signs were being done through the apostles. All who believed were together and had all things in common; they would sell their possessions and goods and distribute the proceeds to all, as any had need. Day by day, as they spent much time together in the temple, they broke bread at home and ate their food with glad and generous hearts, praising God and having the goodwill of all the people. And day by day the Lord added to their number those who were being saved.

What stands out in this description is how the holy and the mundane intermingle. Some of what's described in this passage is holy—the kind of thing that has to do with divine presence. Prayer and praising God, which are religious activities, seem to have been cornerstones of their life together. "Wonders and signs" is another way to talk about miraculous occurrences, and the language of "the Lord added to their number those who were being saved" is a reference to the fact that God was underwriting the flourishing of the apostolic community.

It's clear that this was a religious community and one very much centered on shared experiences of communion with the divine and with each other. But interspersed with these holy references, we find gestures toward everyday life and the intentional ways the apostles organized their community. Notably, this includes a striking communitarianism—a common purpose and well-being. The apostles held things in common, redistributed their wealth according to need, learned in community, and shared meals with each other. It would be difficult to imagine a more idyllic community with more egalitarian values than the one described in the passage above, especially considering the community's recent history of loss and trauma.

The over-the-top way Luke described the apostles' common life has led some interpreters to question whether the portrait in Acts 2:42–47 is historically accurate. After all, if things were happening precisely how this passage suggests, then the apostles would have been living in one of history's great utopian communities or communes, long before that language evolved to describe such situations. And certainly it is possible that the description in Acts 2 is idealized or that it was aspirational—that it was meant to describe the way things *ought* to have been or the way they were *intended* to be, even if the reality did not always measure up. But even if that's true and the portrait here represents a what-if rather than a what-was, it is still an important data point. Even if the community of the apostles never quite reached these levels of harmony and sharing, it is important to notice that they *wanted* to reach them. They *tried* to organize themselves in the kind of radically equal and purposeful community this passage envisions. It's important that they imagined themselves living in this kind of harmony, whether it ever fully materialized or not. That desire for a different kind of community by itself tells us something important about the group's values and desires.

That said, the Acts of the Apostles doesn't offer much evidence to people who want to doubt the historicity of its depictions of the Jerusalem community, as it keeps returning to its descriptions and reiterating just how wonderful and peaceful things were. Check out 4:32–37:

> Now the whole group of those who believed were of one heart and soul, and no one claimed private ownership of any possessions, but everything they owned was held in common. With great power the apostles gave their testimony to the resurrection of the Lord Jesus, and great grace was upon them all. There was not a needy person among them, for as many as owned lands or houses sold them and brought the proceeds of what was sold. They laid it at the apostles' feet, and it was distributed to each as any had need. There was a Levite from Cyprus,

Joseph, to whom the apostles gave the name of Barnabas (which means "son of encouragement"). He sold a field that belonged to him, then brought the money, and laid it at the apostles' feet.

Here, we once again see a description of the Jerusalem apostolic community that emphasizes their common purpose and shared living. The community was organized around shared commitment. In 4:32, the Greek word that's translated as "those who believed" above has the connotation of trust, faithfulness, and commitment. It signals that as a baseline the community was made up of people who shared an investment in the story of Jesus and a different way of living. It's a word that suggests faithfulness and commitment. It's clear that this community was rooted in religious belonging and that its religious belonging found expression in a set of practices: religious practices like giving testimony, yes, but also common ownership of property, communal charity, mutual aid, and radical generosity.

In the Roman Empire, or in any system that insists on hierarchy and demands loyalty to a single leader, this form of living differently would have been its own kind of protest. In our own society today, it would be radical to live this way. The people in the Jerusalem community were simply opting out of the normal patterns of competition and jealous consumption that defined their world. Rather than hoarding possessions for themselves, they gave their stuff away. Rather than jealously guarding what they already had and living in fear of losing their place in the world, Acts describes the people in the community giving up their wealth to help other people. Perhaps that's why the Jerusalem community seems so unbelievable to us today: because we have a hard time imagining anyone voluntarily forfeiting their accumulated possessions and wealth. We have been so conditioned to pile up stuff and money that we cannot enter the headspace of people who decided to give it all up so other people could have enough. At the end of that passage above, Acts lifts up the story of Joseph the Levite from Cyprus, who sells a plot of land and gives the money to the apostles for the common good of the group. What Joseph did was extraordinary, Acts tells us, but it was also ordinary, as it is what almost everyone in the community was doing.

But all is not perfect in the Jerusalem community. Immediately following this passage in Acts 4, we read another story of members of the community selling property, though this one doesn't end so positively. I briefly mentioned this story in the previous chapter of this book, but it's worth revisiting here as a counterexample of how the togetherness and unity of the Jerusalem community worked in practice.

In Acts 5:1–12, a couple named Ananias and Sapphira did the same thing Joseph the Levite from Cyprus did: they sold a piece of property. But in the case of Ananias and Sapphira, Acts says that they "kept back some of the proceeds, and brought only a part and laid it at the apostles' feet" (5:2). This action, as both Jewish tradition and Peter's own words in 5:4 demonstrate, was completely within their rights to do. Jewish tradition held that people should devote a *portion* of their wealth and earnings to God by offering the first fruits of a harvest or a tithe of their income. Here, Ananias and Sapphira did just that. But rather than meeting their generosity with praise, as might be expected, Peter greeted their gift with scorn. "Ananias, why has Satan filled your heart to lie to the Holy Spirit and to keep back part of the proceeds of the land?" (5:3) Ananias was no doubt taken aback.

As Peter continued addressing Ananias (Sapphira was not present for this part of the story), he made it clear that the offense lay not in withholding some of the proceeds but in pretending that the portion that the couple *did* give to the apostles was the whole sum earned from the sale. This seemed to be a violation of trust and breach of some kind of policy, either stated or implicit, that the community had. It also seemed to be a violation of the Holy Spirit's trust. "You did not lie to us but to God!" (5:4) Peter told him, and as he said the words, Ananias fell down and died. Why did Ananias die? Out of fear, shame, regret, or because God killed him as a form of punishment? In any case, when Sapphira came home about three hours later and Peter quizzed her about the price of the property, she too gave the partial figure, and she too fell down and died. "And great fear seized the whole church and all who heard of these things," Acts 5:11 says, and it's not hard to understand why. The togetherness of the community of Jesus-followers was intense and idyllic, but it also seems to have been absolute and rooted in some very strict divine accounting. The episode of Ananias and Sapphira revealed the more difficult side of the Jerusalem community—the consequences for people who agreed to live by the community's values but did not actually follow through. But it also revealed the seriousness with which the community took its own principles.

Another glimpse into the difficulties inherent in living in such a community appears in the very next chapter. Beginning in 6:1 and stretching to verse 4, Acts describes a controversy that breaks out among the members of the community:

> Now during those days, when the disciples were increasing in number, the Hellenists complained against the Hebrews because their widows were being neglected in the daily distribution of food. And the twelve called together the whole community of the disciples and said, "It is not right that we should neglect the word of God in order to wait on tables. Therefore, brothers and sisters, select from among yourselves seven men of good standing, full of the Spirit and of wisdom, whom we

> may appoint to this task, while we, for our part, will devote ourselves to prayer and to serving the word."

Scholars wrestle with how to understand this passage. The labels "Hellenists" and "Hebrews" don't quite work in the context of first-century Judea, especially since they don't really appear elsewhere as descriptions of groups of people in quite this way. But the most common explanation of this conflict is the one that makes the most sense to me: that the Hellenists were Greek-speaking Jews who mostly came from the Jewish diaspora around the Roman Empire and who had moved to Jerusalem from somewhere else. The Hebrews, meanwhile, were likely local Judeans—people who had grown up speaking Aramaic and who had a stronger connection to the local traditions and environments and people. The dispute between the two groups seems to have turned on the question of the charity work made possible by all the sharing that members of the community were doing. The Hellenists' widows, it seems, were not receiving the same amount of aid as the Hebrews' widows.

In the ancient world, widows were among the most vulnerable members of society because their husbands had died and they no longer had a reliable income. Tellingly, widows became very important in the Christian traditions of late antiquity, taking on symbolic power as representatives of the church. But here in Acts, widows seem to have been identified early on as among the kinds of people who could benefit from food aid, which makes sense because one of the major challenges of being a widow would have been finding ways to pay for life's necessities. For whatever reason, the widows who were Hellenists were not receiving the same attention as the ones who were Hebrews. Perhaps it was because the Hellenist widows, having come from somewhere else, did not have the same networks of family and friends to help sustain them, and they consequently fell through the cracks more easily. Or perhaps there was some other reason that we no longer understand. Whatever it was, the matter was serious enough that the Hellenists in the Jerusalem community gathered the whole group to talk it over.

I find the language of 6:2b–4 to be strange. Here, "the twelve" (Jesus' twelve disciples during his lifetime, who were presumably part of the Hebrew faction) seemed to accept the Hellenists' complaints, but they did not accept that they should be the ones to fix it. Rather, "the twelve" invited the Hellenists to nominate their own people to distribute food to their own widows so that the Hebrews did not have to "neglect the word of God to wait on tables." This strikes me as a dismissive way to respond to the Hellenists' very real complaints: by saying that feeding Hellenist widows was beneath them. But the compromise seems to have worked, and the Hellenists chose seven men to do the job, including Stephen, whose stoning becomes a major story in the next few chapters of Acts. The Hellenist widows began to receive distributions of food at the same level that the Hebrew widows did.

This complaint from the Hellenists and the compromise that resolved it tell us that despite the descriptions of the community of believers being "of one heart and soul" and united in their commitment to take care of each other, the community was not always perfect. Conflict arose from time to time, as it does in every community, and accusations of unfairness dogged even this most fair and egalitarian of communities. This story shows that even ideal communities sometimes fail to live up to their values. But this story also shows the Jerusalem community's commitment to its values and the ways it ensured it was living those values by organizing to bring them into reality. It demonstrates that the distribution of food and the broader redistribution of resources was not merely a symbolic gesture meant to signal virtue but an actual social program on which members of the community depended for their material sustenance and well-being. If the distribution had been merely symbolic, then the Hellenist widows might not have objected to unfairness in the way it worked. But because they relied on the food that the community shared in common, they brought the inequality to the attention of the group, and the group addressed it.

It is easy for us to minimize what the community in Jerusalem was trying to achieve. It's easy for us to claim that it could not have been as peaceful, equal, and communal as it is described in the Book of Acts and that the people involved could not really have been as selfless and devoted to each other as the text describes. After all, that is not usually how people behave. But from my perspective, it looks as if the community in Jerusalem really was trying to live out its values by living intentionally in fair and equitable ways. We can tell because of the positive things Acts says about them in places like 2:42–47 and 4:32–37. But we also see evidence of their commitments in passages like 5:1–11, the story of Ananias and Sapphira, and 6:1–7, the story of the Hellenists and the Hebrews, that show the community's conflicts and struggles. The followers of Jesus in Jerusalem seem to have done their best to live purposefully and fairly with each other, in matters both holy and mundane, even when it was difficult.

In autocratic or authoritarian systems that are hierarchical, individualistic, and materialistic and that demand loyalty to and admiration of individual leaders, a way of life like the one described in the early chapters of Acts is a form of protest. In an autocratic system, sharing resources is a form of resistance; and in an empire, being willing to uphold and be upheld by others is radical. When the world around you is authoritarian, depending on violence and coercion to make things happen, a community that works through conversation and consensus—even if it is not always perfect—pushes back against the values of the broader society to live differently. For those of us who find ourselves living in such societies today—societies that value cruelty, selfishness, falsehood, and allegiance to power—the community described in the early chapters of Acts can be an inspiration and a model.

Living in Community in Autocratic Times

If the kind of community described in the early chapters of Acts existed today, we might call it mutual aid. Mutual aid programs emerge within communities to address people's needs. Mutual aid is different from what we find in a capitalist system, in which people need to have or earn the money to purchase things like food, health care, shelter, and education. In a capitalist system, if you don't have the money for those things, you probably won't receive them, except through charity. Mutual aid is also different from charity, which emerges from the inequalities inherent in societies; charity is what we call it when people who have resources give them to people who don't have them. Mutual aid, in contrast, is a voluntary arrangement by which people work together to meet each other's needs. Its premise is sharing without conditions or barriers to participation. In a mutual aid system, people contribute what they can to others and accept what they need from each other, and they collaborate to ensure everyone flourishes.

Such a system may sound idealistic or naïve, especially to those of us who have spent our lives in capitalist systems. After so much time in the competitive, zero-sum world of twentieth- and twenty-first-century America, it can be hard to envision something different. We are used to a system in which not having rent money means you become homeless and not getting health insurance from an employer means you don't get to see a doctor. Most of us have been formed in a society that thinks it's a moral failure not to have enough money to buy groceries and that people should be comfortable taking out tens of thousands of dollars in student loans at eighteen years old. Our own formation in capitalist systems puts a limit on our imagination. When faced with the scenarios I just described, our instinct is to appeal to systems of charity—to ensure that there are homeless shelters, food banks, and that sort of thing—to offer a safety net of last resort. But mutual aid imagines something different: mutual aid intervenes not as a charitable safety net of last resort but as a web of support in meeting life's needs. Mutual aid asks why there should be unhoused people at all, when the world has plenty of housing, or why people should go hungry, when there is plenty of food to go around. In mutual aid, society's problem is not that some individuals fail to find ways to meet their own needs but that all of us fail to live generously with each other and ensure that everyone's needs are met.

There are many models of mutual aid, including governmental ones; some countries set up their governments as a central hub for gathering and distributing resources. But that isn't what things look like for those of us who live in the United States, and that wasn't what things looked like for the community in Jerusalem in the first century. We live—and they lived—in the kind of system that emphasizes the individual's successes or failures and that envisions government as a vehicle for the enrichment of one person or a small class of people. We live in a system that's not so different from the one in Judea in the first century, where people were on their own to make it—or not. Some of us might have resources that can help us out, like families, inherited wealth, or unique talents that are in demand. But at the end of the day, in the United States, most of us are on our own to sink or swim.

In countries like the United States, where there is a weak or absent social safety net, for a long time churches have done the important work of offering food, shelter, education, and health care to people who otherwise wouldn't have it. Christianity (and many other religious communities) can be proud of that. But as we live in a society that has little interest in offering systemic solutions for things like poverty, health and well-being, child care, and education, the Book of Acts offers a vision that's wider even than the one most churches have embraced.

What would it be like to reimagine churches as mutual aid societies? How could we try to live in the kind of intentional community that Acts describes? What if churches understood themselves as something beyond places for worship and charity and instead thought of themselves as hubs for interconnected living and centers for whole communities to thrive together?

As mainline Protestant Christianity faces a steep decline in the United States and other parts of the world, as many churches go looking for ways to repurpose their buildings and their resources for new ways of living, and as our wider society and nation careen toward the hierarchical and selfish ideals of autocracy and authoritarianism, the mutual aid model of Acts might be worth a second look. The aspen trees show us that there is a lot to be said for being connected at the roots.

Further Reading

If you are interested in learning more about mutual aid as a response to the ways our society is organized, you might find www.mutualaidhub.org to be a useful resource. The American Friends Service Committee has a useful guide for thinking about how to create a mutual aid network in your community.[2] And for a longer set of reflections on the patterns of social relation that undergird mutual aid, the book *The Care Manifesto* is a great choice.[3]

One of the most fascinating explorations of how authoritarian and autocratic systems work (and in this particular case, how *fascism* works) is Umberto Eco's 1995 essay "Ur-Fascism." Eco lays out fourteen principles or characteristics of fascism; while not all fascist systems include all the characteristics, all of them include at least some, he says. I'm including the citation for the original publication here, but the article is also freely available on the internet.[4]

[2] Mary Zerkel, "How to Create a Mutual Aid Network," American Friends Service Committee, October 2, 2025, https://afsc.org/news/how-create-mutual-aid-network.

[3] The Care Collective, *The Care Manifesto: The Politics of Interdependence* (Verso, 2020).

[4] Umberto Eco, "Ur-Fascism," *The New York Review of Books* 42, no. 11 (June 22, 1995), https://www.nybooks.com/articles/1995/06/22/ur-fascism/.

10

Togetherness and Inclusion

I already told you that I grew up in a small Southern town. Like many Southern towns, it was racially diverse but very segregated. Not much more than a decade before I started kindergarten, the county school system had become integrated, but only after the usual foot-dragging by officials and activism and protest by citizens—mostly by Black citizens. The tension of desegregation was still palpable when I started school in the early 1980s, though at that age I didn't know what caused the tension or what to call it.

As I grew older, I noticed the way the town organized itself. My family lived in the center of town, where a lot of the White people lived. And on the edges of town, to the northwest and the south, Black families clustered in neighborhoods. The elementary school where I went to the third through sixth grades had been one of the town's Black schools when the system was segregated, so it was located in one of the Black neighborhoods. Though the elementary school was located not more than a mile from our house, it might as well have been in a different town. Driving there each morning and leaving every afternoon, we passed through a neighborhood that we never entered at any other time. I never saw any of the Black kids in my own neighborhood either. We all went to school together every day, but otherwise our social lives were completely separate.

Later, as I began to reflect on my childhood and on the place where I had grown up, I concluded that my hometown had been unusually racially segregated. Not until I moved to other places did I realize that my conclusion was incorrect. My hometown wasn't unusual: it was normal. Elsewhere in the South, in towns like Asheville, Nashville, and Johnson City, I saw the same patterns of segregation, even long after the official forms of Jim Crow had been abolished or diminished. When I moved to Denver and lived outside the South for the first time in my adult life, I felt sure that I would encounter a much more integrated city. I was wrong again. Denver is just as segregated as the other cities I've lived, and it is just as segregated as my tiny hometown.

Though far from the places we tend to associate with the worst of American racism, Colorado has the same divided demographics familiar to me from North Carolina and Tennessee. Neighborhoods that were only a mile or two apart from each other were inhabited by different racial or ethnic groups, with the same "good part of town" and "bad part of town" reputations that people toss around when they talk about race indirectly. With more time I began to understand some of the historical roots of the problem: redlining that sorted people by race, discriminatory lending practices that made it difficult for people of color to buy homes in all-White neighborhoods, and just plain intimidation and white flight. I am struck by how durable the racial divisions are in places as far apart and different as Denver and my own small North Carolina hometown.

The same goes for churches. Martin Luther King Jr.'s famous observation that 11 o'clock on Sunday mornings is the most segregated hour in America still holds true. The Pew Research Center's data show that while some denominations—especially conservative or charismatic ones like the Assemblies of God, the Church of God (Cleveland, Tennessee), and the Churches of Christ—maintain substantial racial diversity, many of the mainline Protestant traditions rank near the bottom of the list.[1] Even within traditions that exhibit some diversity at the national level, individual congregations still tend to be racially homogenous. American congregations mirror the broader American culture and landscape, which has long sorted people by race and ethnicity and which has seen the persistence of segregated social spaces long after official policies of segregation were abolished. American religion bears the marks of American history, which is itself a story of repeated fractures, false starts, incomplete attempts, violent upheavals, and failures of willpower and imagination when it comes to race. Many of the United States' least racially diverse denominations were formed or shaped during the period of slavery and the Civil War, when larger religious movements split into Northern factions and Southern factions and Black factions and White factions. Modern denominations inherit those old divisions, and they perpetuate them too.

I was recently speaking with a congregation on the topic of the apostle Paul and his letters, and as part of that conversation the pastor (a longtime friend of mine) asked what Paul might have to say to American Christians at this point in our history. If we received a letter from Paul, what might be in it? We talked a bit about Martin Luther King Jr.'s famous 1958 sermon "Paul's Letter to American Christians," in which King imagined just such a scenario, a twentieth-century letter from Paul to American Christians. King thought Paul

[1] Michael Lipka, "The Most and Least Racially Diverse U.S. Religious Groups," Pew Research Center, 2015, https://www.pewresearch.org/short-reads/2015/07/27/the-most-and-least-racially-diverse-u-s-religious-groups/.

might say some things about how America's spiritual progress had not kept up with its technological progress, how scientific advances had far outpaced advances in our common humanity.

At least it was possible for King to claim that America was making some small spiritual progress, even if it was too little too slowly. Now it seems America is no longer making any progress whatsoever but is actually going in the wrong direction as regards racial justice and reconciliation and other forms of justice. Instead of the too-slow progress of the 1950s and 1960s, in the 2010s and 2020s we have seen a resurgence of racism and other forms of prejudice and hatred. While it was possible in the mid- to late twentieth century for King to be frustrated that the United States was moving too slowly toward justice, these days are we making any progress at all? We seem to have reversed course and begun moving in the other direction, toward outright hostility and discrimination and forms of open prejudice that had long remained hidden.

If Paul sent a letter to America today, instead of a firm and gentle nudging tone (like King's sermon) or a pleading tone (like many of Paul's letters) it's likely it would include Paul's trademark anger, aimed at the overt racism, rampant sexism and homophobia and transphobia, proud anti-Semitism, naked xenophobia, and out-in-the-open Christian White nationalism so prevalent in the nation and at the highest levels of government. Large swaths of America have abandoned any pretense of togetherness and have instead wholeheartedly and even proudly embraced division and hatred.

The Value of Difference

In chapter 2 I talked about how autocratic leaders and empires use history to justify their actions in the present. By telling the history of the nation in a way that recalls or invents a glorious lost past, autocrats make the case that they alone will be able to restore that past in the future—to make it "great again." This pattern of returning a nation and a people to greatness usually emphasizes the greatness of one group of people over everyone else and therefore puts the restoration of the fortunes of that one group at the center of a possible national resurgence. The rhetoric of national restoration is almost always the rhetoric of ethnic nationalism or racial purity. When history is misused in this way, it is typically to claim that diversity is bad and that some other group of people—foreigners, secret enemies, outsiders, invaders—is trying to bring down the nation and the leader.

In the modern world, this looks like racism and xenophobia. In recent decades, waves of prejudice have swept across the globe. Nationalist movements that have organized against refugee settlement programs and have sparked

Islamophobia are thriving in Europe. Among others, countries such as India, South Africa, and Israel have leveraged claims about history in order to assert the rights or privileges of one group of people over all others. Anti-Semitism is surging in Europe, in the United States, and worldwide. Particularly alarmingly, it is surging especially among young people.[2] The United States is in the throes of its most xenophobic era in modern history and perhaps ever. "All America wants for Christmas is remigration," tweeted the Department of Homeland Security's official X account in December 2025, referring to a form of ethnic cleansing popular in the rhetoric of white nationalist groups (especially in Europe) that seeks to "remigrate" or deport or otherwise expel minorities from the nation. That department has certainly put its power behind its rhetoric, embarking on an alarming program of arrests and deportations, including the arrest and deportation of some people who were legal visitors or residents of the United States or actually U.S. citizens.

Once the framing of belonging shifts to deal in ethnic or racial categories, as the Trump Administration has done, then categories like citizenship no longer matter very much. The government labels anyone who does not fit the racial or ethnic ideal as an outsider and a foreigner and makes them subject to removal, whether they are a citizen or legal resident or not.

Although the values of racism, xenophobia, and ethnic nationalism are now in vogue in the United States and around the world, many of us remember a different set of commitments. These commitments are often called "diversity, equity, and inclusion," or DEI for short, and they have become forbidden ideas and dirty words in the United States under Trump. The principle behind diversity, equity, and inclusion is that we are better when we are together, not when we are segregated by race or ethnicity or some other category. Furthermore, when we practice diversity, equity, and inclusion, we often find that our unity is improved by treating one another with mutual respect and generosity. Many corporations and organizations have implemented DEI policies because of the positive effect they have on the effectiveness of the organization. Employees, customers, and community members are happier and more productive when everyone is included and everyone feels respected. It is telling that as one of their first acts repressive regimes often roll back such programs of inclusion and equity and insist that the nation exists only for the benefit of a select group of people.

Thinking in terms of systems of government, we have already seen that autocratic, authoritarian, and nationalist governments often denounce DEI

---

[2] Yair Rosenberg, "'The More I'm Around Young People, the More Panicked I Am,'" *The Atlantic*, December 15, 2025, https://www.theatlantic.com/ideas/2025/12/american-anti-semitism-youth/685261/.

practices and embrace a more exclusionary vision of the nation's history and its future. Authoritarian and autocratic leaders often emphasize the purity or true belonging of a small subset of the population over and above the belonging of others (typically immigrants, ethnic or racial minorities, gendered or sexual minorities), whom it identifies as outsiders. A similar but opposed pattern also holds true in democracies; democratic systems often find practices of inclusion to be amenable to their values and embrace them. If, like me, you grew up in public school civics and history classes, then you probably heard a version of "America is a melting pot." Whatever the limitations of that metaphor and whatever ways America has failed to live it out completely in practice, the impulse behind it makes sense: America, as a democratic state, has long thought of itself as a place of inclusion, diversity, and equity: a place where differences can be celebrated but where those differences also melt away as we find common ways to belong together. Even if those things have never been perfectly true about the country, it has been the idea we have taught to schoolchildren as a fundamental characteristic of the nation.

Togetherness—the values of inclusion and equity and diversity—was also a hallmark of the early community of Jesus-followers as the Book of Acts describes. Although it's an anachronistic and misplaced description in many ways, Acts described the community in Jerusalem in democratic terms: as a place where belonging was available to many kinds of people. In the midst of an autocratic world that told individuals to look after their own well-being, the community in Jerusalem chose to live differently as interconnected and mutually responsible to each other. As we live into an age of increased ethnic nationalism, pushback against DEI initiatives, and overt racism and xenophobia, the practices of that Jerusalem community have some important lessons to teach us. Let's turn to them now.

Togetherness and Inclusion in Acts

All the way back in the introduction to this book, I mentioned that while I learned about the existence of the Book of Acts when I was a kid, I never learned much about it or about the stories in it. One big exception was the story of Pentecost, which is found in Acts chapter 2. The story of Pentecost is memorable, action-packed, and one-of-a-kind in the Bible, and it helps to tell the story of an important theological concept for many Christians: the Trinity. For Christians who see and understand God in three persons—Father (or Creator), Son, and Spirit—the Pentecost, with its narrative of the arrival of the Holy Spirit, is a triumphant and energizing story. Many Christian congregations celebrate Pentecost with a special day of wearing red to symbolize the "divided tongues, as of fire" that rested on each of the apostles' heads at the arrival of the Holy Spirit, and those churches often celebrate Pentecost as the day when the church was born. Pentecost, for many Christians, tells the story of how and why the church exists at all and the spark of unity that brought the church together.

In chapter 3 of this book I talked about the Pentecost story and how its narrative pushed back on the Roman Empire's hunger for territory. I talked about how the list of identities in Acts 2:9–11 mirrored and undermined the Empire's expansive geographical vision. The story of Pentecost is told in a manner that plays on imperial expectations and complicates them, setting the Jesus Movement against the Roman Empire as a counterbalancing force and placing the Jesus Movement within the Roman Empire as a form of resistance to its power. But there's another related and important aspect to the story of Pentecost as it appears in Acts: Pentecost announced the community that gathered around Jesus as a multi-ethnic, multi-national, expansive, and inclusive movement. After the day of Pentecost, which took place right at the beginning of Acts, it was no longer possible to view the Jesus Movement as a provincial or parochial concern limited to one group of people or to one vision of the world. After Pentecost, the church was born as a place where many kinds of difference come together.

Recall that only a few verses before the story of Pentecost, in Acts 1:6–8, Jesus had promised the arrival of the Holy Spirit. Jesus' words came in response to a question from the disciples. The disciples had asked Jesus whether the moment had arrived when he would restore the kingdom to Israel, when Jesus would take up the throne of David and turn Israel into a powerful and proud nation. In essence, Jesus' response was to say, *No—that is not what is happening right now*. Instead, Jesus said in that moment, "You will receive power when the Holy Spirit has come upon you, and you will be my witnesses in Jerusalem, in all Judea and Samaria, and to the ends of the earth." The arrival of the Holy Spirit, Jesus was saying, would signal not the concentration of God's presence into one nation in one place but the infusion of God's presence into *all* people and places. The promise of witnessing "to the ends of the earth" must have sounded grandiose and unattainable to the people standing there on that day.

Only a chapter later, Jesus' words began to take on a tangible shape. Once the Holy Spirit arrived in wind and flame on the day of Pentecost, the first thing the Spirit did was give the apostles the ability to bridge differences. "Now there were devout Jews from every people under heaven living in Jerusalem," Acts 2:5–11 begins.

> And at this sound the crowd gathered and was bewildered, because each one heard them speaking in the native language of each. Amazed and

astonished, they asked, "Are not all these who are speaking Galileans? And how is it that we hear, each of us, in our own native language? Parthians, Medes, Elamites, and residents of Mesopotamia, Judea and Cappadocia, Pontus and Asia, Phrygia and Pamphylia, Egypt and the parts of Libya belonging to Cyrene, and visitors from Rome, both Jews and proselytes, Cretans and Arabs—in our own languages we hear them speaking about God's deeds of power."

This passage is told as a story about language, a story of how each person who was present there on the day of Pentecost heard the apostles speaking in their own language, even though the apostles did not know how to speak all of those languages. But while language is important in the story, language here is standing in for a much broader idea with much larger implications. The day of Pentecost was not announcing the arrival of some kind of real-time translation tool; this was not a neat trick to make communication easier. Yes, on the surface, Pentecost was a story about language. But more deeply it was a story about peoplehood. In Acts 2:5 the NRSVue refers to "every people under heaven," where "people" is a translation of the Greek word *ethnos*. *Ethnos* refers to a *people*, as the NRSVue rightly translates it, or a *nation*, bound together by kinship, tradition, and shared language and culture. It's the root of our modern English words *ethnic* and *ethnicity*, which refer to how different people-groups belong together. The same was true in the ancient world. All the people present there on that day of Pentecost belonged to Judaism in some broad sense. They were all "devout Jews from every people under heaven," after all, even if some of them were gentile converts to Judaism, as 2:10 points out. But even though they were all part of the Jewish people, they also belonged to distinct peoples elsewhere—to ethnicities and nations scattered all over the Mediterranean basin, across and even beyond the Roman Empire. They came from all over to visit Jerusalem for the festival of Pentecost, but they brought their distinct cultures, traditions, and languages with them.

Here, at the beginning of the Jesus Movement, the story of Pentecost was defining the church as a collection of people bonded in togetherness despite their differences. The story of Pentecost began in diversity and difference, and it ended in understanding and commonality. Pentecost shifted the apostles' expectations away from the restoration of one nation's political power and toward the establishment of a community that transcended many kinds of difference, offering a form of belonging that was not rooted in ethnicity, political affiliation, or race. Pentecost set the agenda for the Jesus Movement (what we now call Christianity) as an inclusive and diverse collection of people, united across differences in pursuit of common values.

It didn't take long for that unity and inclusion to be put to the test. Already in an earlier chapter we talked about the story of Peter and Cornelius. To review briefly, Cornelius was a "centurion of the Italian Cohort," a high-ranking Roman soldier who was part of the occupying military presence stationed in Caesarea to prevent any possible Judean rebellion. Cornelius was, therefore, a gentile, meaning a non-Jewish person. Whereas the group collected at the day of Pentecost all had been Jews (including a few Roman proselytes to Judaism), here in Acts 10 the story of Cornelius posed a question to the movement, asking how seriously it took its principles of inclusion. Cornelius was "a devout man who feared God," 10:2 tells us, but he was not a Jewish convert. Cornelius was a gentile, and more than that, he was the kind of person many Judeans would have considered an enemy because his very existence in Caesarea signified the ongoing Roman occupation of their land and the subjugation of their people. Cornelius was in Judea as an agent of an oppressive regime.

Tellingly, it is God who brought Cornelius and Peter together. Both men received visons, separately, preparing them for their encounter. Cornelius' vision, related in 10:3–6, told him to send for Peter and ask to have a conversation. Peter's vision, related in 10:11–16, is a bit stranger. In a "trance," Peter had a vision of a sheet being lowered to the ground by its four corners. The sheet was filled with all kinds of animals—a very odd thing to imagine and a strange vision to receive. A voice told Peter to kill the animals and eat them, but in the vision Peter objected on the basis of Jewish dietary laws, which restrict the kinds of animals that Jews are supposed to treat as food. Then the voice responded, saying, "What God has made clean, you must not call profane." As Peter was coming out of his trance, the men sent by Cornelius arrived to summon him, and the next day Peter went with them to the house of Cornelius. When he arrived, Peter referred to his takeaway from his vision, in 10:28. "You yourselves know that it is improper for a Jew to associate with or to visit an outsider," he said, "but God has shown me that I should not call anyone profane or unclean"—even a Roman soldier. Peter stayed with Cornelius for several days, baptizing him and others, and the whole lot of them were united in community. The way the story is told, Peter heard from God that his specific forms of belonging (the dietary rules included in the Jewish law) should not stand in the way of broader forms of belonging, meaning he could eat with someone like Cornelius even if that entailed moving beyond the boundaries of what, where, and with whom Jews were supposed to eat.

We should be careful when reading passages like this as gentile Christians in the twenty-first century. There is a long history of Christians misinterpreting passages like this one and of misunderstanding and misrepresenting the Jewish tradition as an especially exclusionary or prejudiced thing. Christians have seized on passages like this one to argue that Judaism was (and is) a religion that isolates itself, looks down on others, and seeks separation from "unclean" gentiles. But we should remember that Acts and the rest of the New Testament are books written from the perspective of Jewish followers of Jesus and that they do not always represent Jews and Judaism as a whole, how all Jewish people would have represented themselves, or the way a neutral observer would. While some Jews might have held the attitude Peter described and argued for a strict separation from gentiles, there is plenty of evidence from a variety of sources that most Jews in most places had regular and close contact with gentiles and that there was nothing especially unusual about Jews among the other peoples of the ancient world. It's possible to read too much into Peter's words here in Acts 10, and it's definitely possible to be too confident when using this part of Acts to describe all of ancient or modern Judaism.

The point here is not that Judaism was or was not, and is or is not, a community with strict boundaries. The point is that the Jews who made up the earliest parts of the Jesus Movement (Jews like Jesus, Peter, Paul, and others) quickly came to understand diversity in their movement to be a powerful tool and symbol. Already by the first century there was a long history of Jews understanding that the God of Israel was the God of the whole world, and many Jews expected that eventually the gentiles would come to understand that. Just look at Peter's citation of the prophet Joel, for example, in his speech on the day of Pentecost in 2:17–21, where he quotes a centuries-old prophetic book to say that God's spirit will be poured out "upon all flesh," not just Jews, and that "everyone who calls on the name of the Lord shall be saved," not just Israel itself.

Peter's fellowship with Cornelius and other gentiles is a concrete expression of a very old Jewish idea: that God is the God of everyone. As it turns out, precisely this tension played out in Peter's report to the other apostles in Jerusalem after he returned from Cornelius' house. Some of the apostles challenged Peter, asking how he could have dined at the same table with "uncircumcised" people who did not keep the law of Moses regarding food purity. In response, Peter told the story of his trance and his experiences with Cornelius and the others, and by the end of their exchange, in 11:18, the apostles were saying that "God has given even to the gentiles the repentance that leads to life." As the Jesus Movement began to coalesce and establish its way of relating to the world, in this story and in others it embraced togetherness and unity in diversity as ways of responding to the work of the Holy Spirit.

The question arose again in chapter 15 of Acts, when the apostles and other members of the community again got into a disagreement about the church's engagement with gentiles. Through a series of conversations and eventually a large meeting in Jerusalem, the group worked through the question of whether someone needed to follow Jewish law (including, critically, circumcision and adherence to the whole of the Mosaic law) to be a follower of Jesus. This meeting, often anachronistically called the "Council of Jerusalem" to place it at the head of a long church tradition of ecumenical councils, ended up reaffirming that gentiles can become followers of Jesus without first having to satisfy all the requirements of Jewish observance. The group drafted a letter to gentile followers of Jesus to outline their decision, with the provision (preserved in Acts 15:29) that gentiles should "abstain from what has been sacrificed to idols and from blood and from what is strangled and from sexual immorality." This outcome represented a compromise of sorts, likely giving both sides of the debate something they could claim as a victory. But in the end, the solution once more left the door wide open to the gentiles, and it pointed to inclusion and togetherness as the guiding principles of the movement.

We saw in the previous chapter of this book that the community of early Jesus-followers in Jerusalem was not perfect, that it sometimes experienced conflicts and disputes, for example. The most prominent of these conflicts, as we saw, was the tension between the "Hellenist" and "Hebrew" factions of Jewish followers of Jesus when it came to the distribution of food to the community's widows. In Acts 6:1–6, the Hellenists complained that their own widows were not receiving as much benefit as the widows from the Hebrew community. It is not completely clear whom these labels represented, but it's likely that "Hebrew" and "Hellenist" were ways of describing places of birth and therefore cultural and linguistic affiliations. The Hellenists were probably Jews from the diaspora, people born and raised outside of Judea who spoke Greek as their first language, and the Hebrews were likely locals whose first language was Aramaic. If that's true, then this tension represents another example of the kinds of conflicts that difference can introduce. It would have been easy, at a moment like this, for the community to fracture around ethnic, linguistic, and cultural differences. Instead, the Jerusalem community once more reaffirmed its commitment to unity across difference. The Jerusalem community dealt with the controversy between the Hebrews and the Hellenists by coming together, naming their disagreements and differences, and working to find a solution that ensured all members of the community received what they needed.

Perhaps the most powerful and dramatic example of the early Jesus Movement's commitment to togetherness across difference comes in chapter 8 of Acts, when the apostle Philip encountered the Ethiopian eunuch on the road from Jerusalem to Gaza. In Acts 8:26–40, an angel told Philip to go to the road to Gaza, which ran through a desert wilderness area. Philip did as the angel told him, and when he got to the wilderness road, he encountered a court official from Ethiopia, a eunuch who was the treasurer for an Ethiopian called the Candace, who was the queen of that people.

Scholars have noticed how the Ethiopian eunuch represents a great many kinds of differences. Ethiopia was geographically distant from the area where most of Acts takes place, and it was not part of the Roman Empire. The Ethiopian was a eunuch, meaning he likely had been castrated as a child in preparation for service in a royal court. That castration signifies violence and perhaps slavery, and certainly eunuchs in the ancient world represented sexual and gender difference. Furthermore, and perhaps surprisingly, the chariot and the scroll suggest that the Ethiopian had a high status and access to a great deal of wealth. Scholars note that as an Ethiopian, the eunuch would have had dark skin. While skin color held different symbolism in the ancient world than it does in the modern world, the eunuch's skin color still would have stood out as a form of difference from many people in the Roman world.[3] The journey to Jerusalem and possessing the Isaiah scroll also suggest that the Ethiopian might have been Jewish, or at least interested and invested in the Jewish people and the Jewish God. Taken together, these many different markers and descriptions of identity and status portray the Ethiopian eunuch in a fascinating and diverse array of ways: he was both privileged and subjugated, both subjected to violence and also powerful, both pious and curious and something of a seeker.

Why does Acts tell this story? In chapter 3 of this book, I mentioned that perhaps Luke was pointing to Ethiopia as one of the places where Jesus' promise of "to the ends of the earth" would become a reality, since Ethiopia was about as far away as the Roman imagination could travel. Perhaps by encountering the Ethiopian, Philip ensured that witness about Jesus would move far afield just as Jesus predicted, and by being baptized the Ethiopian became the vessel by which that witness would move. But that geographical purpose could have been accomplished with a much simpler character than the Ethiopian eunuch; it was not necessary, narratively speaking, to make the Ethiopian so representative of so many different forms of difference. Luke could have told the story of the spread of the Jesus Movement with a plainer character or without a character at all. Luke could have said simply that the message of Jesus had spread as far as Ethiopia.

Modern scholars have noted that the Ethiopian eunuch stands in for sexual and gender diversity, for racial and ethnic diversity, for geographical diversity,

---

[3] See many of the essays in Nasrallah and Schüssler Fiorenza's volume: Laura Nasrallah and Elizabeth Schüssler Fiorenza, eds., *Prejudice and Christian Beginnings: Investigating Race, Gender, and Ethnicity in Early Christian Studies* (Fortress Press, 2010).

and for economic diversity and that the story Acts tells would be much flatter and less expansive without the Ethiopian's presence.

Things like gender, ethnicity, class, and territory do not simply represent modern concerns, either. The dizzying variety of ways Acts 8:16–40 describes the Ethiopian would likewise have struck ancient readers as reflecting the identities of many kinds of people, including identities from the margins of society, the Roman Empire, and the known world (from the Roman point of view). The Ethiopian's story (which is a story of devotion, piety, faithfulness, and holy curiosity) found a place in the Book of Acts because it fits thematically with how the rest of Acts describes the early Jesus Movement. Acts tells the story of the Jesus Movement as a home for people from diverse backgrounds, as a community of inclusion that practices togetherness across difference.

Living Togetherness

In systems that demand sameness, that privilege ethnic and racial purity, and that seek to segregate people from each other, one of the most radical things you can do is live in community across differences and across boundaries. When your society is telling you to love only the people who are exactly like you and hate or reject everyone who is different, the very act of creating community and connection can be revolutionary. That's what I remember thinking and feeling as a kid in the newly desegregated schools of my small Southern hometown learning about America as a "melting pot": that for all its flaws and failures America was supposed to be the kind of place where we could belong together across our differences. I remember buying into the idea that my country is the sort of place where desegregation is a step in the right direction, where the passage of time always brings us closer to the ideal of a nation in which our differences matter less than the things we have in common. Now, as an adult, I can see how that idea was flawed and naïve and how a White kid like me could have believed it more easily than my Black classmates. But at least it was an idea we said out loud about ourselves, even if we didn't always live up to it. I can remember some of the songs we sang on Wednesday nights at the Southern Baptist church across the street from our house. "Red and yellow, Black and White," we sang, in the way of describing racial diversity that might make us cringe now but was remarkable for the time and place, "they are precious in his sight, Jesus loves the little children of the world." Even though every seven-year-old in that room was White, that song taught us that diversity and inclusion matter and that Jesus loves everyone the same.

Stephen Miller (deputy chief of staff and homeland security advisor in the second Trump Administration and the architect of many of the administration's schemes to imprison and deport migrants) sometimes mockingly refers to diversity as "the national religion."[4] By putting it that way, Miller is pointing to precisely the kind of togetherness I learned in elementary school and through the songs we sang at our Southern Baptist church. By describing America's "religion" of diversity that way, Miller means to cast himself as a kind of heretic—as someone who sees through the national orthodoxy of inclusion and melting-pot togetherness and understands truth differently or better than the rest of us. In a biography of Miller written at the end of the first Trump Administration, when Miller was already a prominent and influential figure and an architect of the policy of separating families at the southern U.S. border, journalist and biographer Jean Guerrero digs into Miller's childhood and education to get a sense of how he arrived at his ideas.[5] Guerrero describes Miller's childhood in posh and liberal Santa Monica, California, and how Miller came to reject the "national religion" of diversity and instead embrace a form of white supremacist and white nationalist politics. She tells the story of how Miller abruptly told a Mexican-American middle school friend that they would not be friends anymore, citing the friend's Latino heritage. She relates how in high school and college Miller would throw trash on the ground and loudly remark to anyone who would listen that it was the job of the janitors (who were non-White people) to pick it up. She describes his meteoric rise to the top of the American conservative movement and his influence on that movement as it became increasingly anti-diversity and pro-White. If diversity is the American "national religion," as Miller puts it, then Miller is determined to purge that national religion and to instill a new one that puts the interests of White Americans first.

Stephen Miller's views are extreme, even within the Trump Administration, but he is far from alone in his vision for America. The Trump Administration has turned the full resources of the federal government to pursuing Miller's goals. It has canceled government grants that mention diversity, equity, and inclusion, and it has purged mentions of those things from government websites and documents. ProPublica found that in response to the Trump Administration's efforts at the government level, over a thousand nonprofit groups and other organizations have removed the language of DEI from their own mission statements and public documents.[6] Meanwhile, government agencies like ICE continue targeting non-White people, including legal residents and citizens, and

---

[4] "Stephen Miller," Southern Poverty Law Center, accessed December 19 2025, https://www.splcenter.org/resources/extremist-files/stephen-miller/.

[5] Jean Guerrero, *Hatemonger: Stephen Miller, Donald Trump, and the White Nationalist Agenda* (William Morrow, 2020).

[6] Ellis Simani, "Under Trump, More Than 1,000 Nonprofits Strip DEI Language from Tax Forms," *ProPublica*, December 17, 2025, https://www.propublica.org/article/deleting-dei-language-nonprofits-irs-forms.

prestigious universities have closed down longstanding academic departments and other programs that study non-White cultures.[7] If diversity really is the "national religion," as Miller says, then America is in a time of unprecedented apostasy.

One of the clearest lessons of the Book of Acts is that when an authoritarian state demands allegiance and tries to privilege one group of people above all the rest, the only proper response is to invest in diversity and inclusion. The story of Pentecost, so central to the faith of so many Christians, is a story about divine inclusion and the radical togetherness that comes through community. The Book of Acts goes out of its way to tell the story of the Ethiopian eunuch, and it is a story of differences and diversities piled up. It's the story of someone from the margins of the world and the margins of society who found welcome in the community of the followers of Jesus. Peter, in his vision from God, learned that God never stands in the way of different kinds of people unifying but indeed always rejoices in moments of inclusion. Diversity might be America's "national religion" (though not for long, if Stephen Miller is to be believed), but the Book of Acts tells us that diversity and togetherness are how God wants the world to be. And that remains true, no matter what any autocrat might have to say about it.

Further Reading

Here I can give no better recommendation than the one I gave early in this book, which is to pick up Willie James Jennings' commentary on Acts.[8] In it, you'll find a lot of wise words that say better than I can how Acts points to flourishing communities based on mutuality and divine togetherness. As Jennings puts it at the beginning of the introduction to his book, "Acts speaks of revolution. We must never forget this."

---

[7] Emma Whitford, "UNC to Close Area Studies Centers," *Inside Higher Ed*, December 19, 2025, https://www.insidehighered.com/news/quick-takes/2025/12/19/unc-close-area-studies-centers.

[8] Willie James Jennings, *Acts: A Theological Commentary on the Bible* (Westminster John Knox, 2017).

CONCLUSION

11

By What Power

"By what power or by what name did you do this?" the council asked John and Peter in the fourth chapter of Acts.

The two apostles were standing in the midst of what we might call a preliminary hearing, having been arrested in the temple a day earlier and having spent the previous night in jail. Peter and John had been teaching in the Jerusalem temple, holding forth to the crowds about the resurrection of the dead, Acts tells us, and a group of leaders confronted them. A group of "priests, the captain of the temple, and the Sadducees"—in short, the ones vested with authority over the Jerusalem temple and its functioning—intervened in John and Peter's preaching and took them into custody. And now the apostles were being made to answer for their actions. "By what power" did Peter and John speak, the leaders wanted to know. By what authority did they act?

Although this episode in Acts 4 played out in a local council and involved more religious than civil matters, the leaders' question—"By what power or by what name did you do this?"—runs through the whole of Luke's narrative. From city streets to marketplaces, from palaces to courtrooms, from prison cells to roadsides, and all the way to Rome itself, the question of power and authority courses through the Book of Acts. Acts threads the story of Jesus' first followers through the fabric of Roman power, telling how the first Christians created a radical and lasting new community in the shadow of one of history's most powerful empires. Luke paints a detailed picture of life under autocracy, showing us how leaders can be corrupt, how many are more concerned with protecting money than protecting people, how empires covet and rule far-flung territories to extract their wealth, how history and peoplehood can be twisted into engines of power, how violence hovers over everything, and how communities can face all the conditions of authoritarian rule and still choose to live differently. "By what power or by what name did you do this?" is a good question—and a dangerous one—when you are living in systems that hoard power and demand obedience.

The Book of Acts and the Conditions and Strategies of Autocracy and Empire

The people we meet in the Book of Acts all lived under the conditions of autocracy. With a few exceptions (like the Parthians in the story of Pentecost and the Ethiopian eunuch), they were all subject to the Roman Empire, even if they occupied radically different positions within it. Everyone in the story lived with an awareness of how power shaped what was possible and impossible in their lives.

Many of the specific circumstances we find in Acts turn out to be general characteristics of living under autocracies. In the beginning of this book, for example, we saw how the Roman system of governance allowed and even encouraged corruption—how figures like Claudius Lysias, Felix, and Festus leveraged the power of their positions for personal gains of some kind. In chapter 3 we saw how history was twisted and construed to support certain kinds of claims in the present—to "Make Ephesus Great Again," for example, or to police the boundaries of Roman-ness by casting outsiders as threats. In chapter 4 we saw how empires covet territory and use it to draw resources from the periphery to the center, and we saw how Judea was one of those peripheral places from the perspective of the people at the center of Roman power. And in chapter 5 we saw how the Book of Acts describes its own heroes as figures living on the edges of power, on the outside of culture and respect.

The middle part of this book catalogued some of the strategies autocracies and empires use. In chapter 5 we saw how criminal justice systems in Acts were not designed to deliver justice, but rather to reinforce the structures and systems of power that were already in place. Relatedly, in chapter 6 we noticed how imprisonment in the Book of Acts describes an unfair and confusing system by which the Roman Empire stripped Paul of his freedom and turned him into a pawn in other people's games. In chapter 7 we saw how violence and the threat of violence show up again and again in Acts as a tool of control, and in chapter 9 we noted how the characters in Acts often protected money above people.

Not all of these conditions and strategies found in the Book of Acts were the direct actions of the autocrat, Caesar. In fact, almost none of them were. Instead, the system itself or people who were part of the autocratic system undertook the many exercises of power found in the Book of Acts. Autocracy and authoritarianism don't mean that one person does all the bad stuff; autocracy and authoritarianism mean that the normal functioning of society and government becomes so twisted by the demands and desires of one person that the whole system and everyone in it begin to behave in unjust ways. Felix was not Caesar, but because of the way Caesar acted and because no one held Felix accountable, Felix kept Paul locked in prison for two years in the hopes of receiving a bribe. Caesar didn't show up in Acts 16, but the owners of the enslaved girl were able to rouse a mob and bring Paul and Silas before the city authorities. They accused the apostles of being foreigners and of violating the city's customs and Roman norms—even though that was not their real grievance with Paul and Silas—because the conditions of autocracy made xenophobia and economic protectionism into powerful arguments. Jesus' death set the stage for Acts, Paul's death looms invisible beyond the book's ending, and several other deaths and brushes with violence pervade the story, showing how violence is an ever-present fact of life in a system founded on coercion and force.

In autocratic and authoritarian systems like the one found in the Book of Acts, it doesn't take a single strongman to do all the bad things. Instead, the whole system becomes corrupted by example and by the leader's permission and even encouragement to behave without constraints and restraint. Peter and John weren't detained by Romans in chapter 4, and Stephen wasn't stoned to death by Romans in chapter 7. Instead, the violence and domination of the system gave others permission to act in violent and dominating ways. Throughout Acts, people join mobs, make dishonest claims, twist history to their purposes, protect money, and participate in corrupt systems of justice because life under autocracy made all of those things not only possible but permissible, and in some cases even praiseworthy.

Twenty-First-Century America and the Conditions and Strategies of Autocracy and Empire

In this book I have talked about several autocrats: Ferdinand Marcos, Vladimir Putin, and Narendra Modi, to name a few. I could have named plenty of others, too—Fidel Castro, Nicolás Maduro, and Iran under its supreme leaders. I have talked about authoritarian systems and systems that exhibit some of the characteristics of authoritarianism, like apartheid-era South Africa and China during the Tiananmen Square protests, and I also could have included others like Afghanistan under Taliban rule and Turkey over the past couple of decades. The world is full of autocrats, and there is no shortage of authoritarian regimes.

But as I was writing this book and envisioning the people who would read it, I worked with one particular autocrat in mind and with one specific form of authoritarianism informing me most strongly: President Donald Trump in the United States, and especially the government he has formed and overseen in his second presidential term.

As I worked on this book, I often found myself pausing to ask whether I have been too forceful or not forceful enough about certain claims. Are the actions of ICE in rounding people up and imprisoning them without trial the kind of thing an authoritarian state would do? I think the answer is clearly yes, but I can imagine that others might disagree. Does the rhetoric of "Make America Great Again" signal a reframing of history, the way autocracies often do? I am confident that it does, but others would push back. Do stark disparities in policing and incarceration signal that U.S. criminal justice operates with a systemic racial bias? The work of Michelle Alexander and others tells me that's obviously true, but not everyone would accept that conclusion. After all, some people claimed (without much evidence or analysis) that the administrations of presidents like Barack Obama and Joe Biden were authoritarian or even fascist. I have asked myself along the way whether it is possible that I am simply labeling people with whom I disagree and seeing patterns that are not really there.

I suppose anything is possible, but I have written this book the way I have because I am convinced that the United States under Donald Trump is sliding rapidly toward authoritarianism or is already there. The Supreme Court has consistently expanded the role of the presidency as Trump has requested. The Trump Administration has lodged criminal charges against its perceived enemies and has squeezed universities to make changes by threatening their funding. The Trump Administration has gutted many federal agencies and the federal workforce despite a lack of clarity about whether it was legally permitted to do so. Though clearly illegal, ICE agents continue to process people for imprisonment and deportation without trials. Trump and his family members have profited from business arrangements with many foreign firms and nations (as much as four billion dollars as of early 2026, according to some reports), which is a violation of the emoluments clause of the Constitution and several federal laws.[1] And Trump has unilaterally imposed tariffs on dozens of countries, though legally the power to impose tariffs rests with Congress. He has fired members of independent agencies established by Congress despite lacking the authority to do so. Airstrikes on purported drug-smuggling boats continue in the Caribbean despite such strikes being illegal and immoral, and as of this writing dozens or even hundreds of people—smugglers or not—have been killed without trial or the opportunity to defend themselves. Trump has

---

[1] "How the Presidency Is Making Trump Richer," NPR, February 8, 2026, https://www.npr.org/transcripts/nx-s1-5704312.

deployed the National Guard to cities with whose leadership he disagrees, and he has restored statues devoted to the Confederacy. I could go on.

The point is not whether I agree or disagree with the actions in that last paragraph, though I disagree with them all. The point is that in both his terms as president, especially the second, President Trump has seized more and more power for himself, disregarded laws and limits on his authority, and turned the office of the presidency into a piggy bank for his own benefit and the benefit of friends and family. The point is that he uses violence and the apparatus of the state against people he does not like (such as immigrants, non-White people, prosecutors and investigators who charged him with things or accused him of things in the past). The point is that Trump shows all the hallmarks of an autocrat and authoritarian, like denigrating the free press, demonizing minorities, and proclaiming demonstrable falsehoods as if they were gospel truth. I have written this book this way because I am convinced that, like the people we meet in the Book of Acts, we are living under the power of an autocratic regime and we are increasingly subject to the power of an authoritarian state.

So How Are We to Live?

In chapters 9 and 10, we saw how the first followers of Jesus responded to the conditions of autocracy and empire. Faced with living under Roman rule, with all its plunder and violence and oppression, the earliest followers of Jesus chose to live differently. They opted out of the injustice of the world around them as much as possible, and when it came to how they understood themselves and their calling from God, they took a different approach. While it might have been easier for them to accept Caesar's ways and join in the rampant marginalization, bias, and theft of their world, members of the early church took a different path.

The earliest Christians valued community. They held things in common, which was a way to push back against the pressure to be self-centered and to treat everyone else like an enemy. They took care of each other, ensuring that the most vulnerable people among them had enough. The early church engaged in mutual aid, setting up systems that guaranteed the dignity of everyone. In a world dominated by individuality and greed, they chose mutuality, commonality, and sharing.

The earliest Christians also valued diversity. Although it's a "bad" word these days under Trump, diversity is woven through the story Acts tells. From the very beginnings of the book in the story of Pentecost to the story of the Ethiopian eunuch to the story of Cornelius and Peter and the formation of community across differences, the Book of Acts wants us to know that the story of Christianity is the story of inclusion. Acts goes out of its way to show that following Jesus means building a community across differences and including the full diversity of human beings. Only a few sentences into the Book of Acts in 1:6, the disciples ask Jesus whether they are witnessing the restoration of one nation—the moment when Jesus would "Make Israel Great Again." *No*, Jesus says, *that's not why we are here, and that is not the moment we are witnessing.* Instead, Jesus tells them, they will receive power and they will be witnesses to that power to the ends of the earth. That witness is about a different way to live—a way to live in community, across different kinds of diversity, and in the power of the Holy Spirit. That witness is about inclusion. That witness is the answer to the question Peter and John are asked in chapter 4 of Acts: "By what power or by what name" did the apostles live? Their power, it turns out, is the power of God and the power of people to choose community over division, diversity over exclusion, love over hatred, and togetherness over the world's many forms of division.

Postscript

I hit *send* on the manuscript for this book on January 5, 2026, only a handful of days into the second calendar year of the second Trump Administration. As I drafted the book in late 2025, I holed up in a little house on the water and spent every day writing and watching shorebirds play out their dramas: terns and gulls and pelicans and the occasional wayward loon, all jostling for space on the beach and keeping a keen eye out for fish. Sometimes, when I was thinking about the central place of the sea in the latter chapters of the Book of Acts, I wondered if Paul noticed the same kinds of birds on his journey to Rome or during his time shipwrecked on the island of Malta. Other times, I found myself reflecting on the way the water alternated between quiet and loud, between flat and whitecapped, between peaceful and stormy. In the background, the whole time I was drafting this book and watching the birds' turf wars, I was noticing the way the news cycled and alternated too, from storm to calm and back again, lurching from one story to the next, a new outrage at breakfast forgotten by lunch. It was hard to escape the connections between what I was writing and what was going on in the world around me, and it was hard to avoid the conclusion that in the months between finishing the book and seeing it published, a lot was going to happen. A lot was going to change.

The publisher agreed, and we decided that here, at the end of this book, we would include an update. We were sure that the book would need one by the time it was published, nearly a year later. Unfortunately, we were absolutely correct.

As I put the finishing touches on this book manuscript, the United States launched a military operation in Venezuela, bombing air defenses and storming the president's residence in Caracas. The United States arrested Venezuelan President Nicolás Maduro and his wife, Cilia Flores, and spirited them away to jails in New York to face drug trafficking charges, a stunning breach of international norms. The United States has since behaved like an imperial force in Venezuela: installing a loyal government, seizing control of the country's oil industry, and treating a sovereign nation like a client state. Secretary of State Marco Rubio is now widely understood to control Venezuela's economy and government.[1]

[1] Tyler Pager and Anatoly Kurmanaev, "How Marco Rubio is Running Venezuela from Afar," *New York Times*, July 11, 2026, https://www.nytimes.com/2026/07/11/us/politics/how-marco-rubio-runs-venezuela.html?smid=url-share.

A few days after the invasion of Venezuela, ICE agents—which had been swarming Minneapolis as part of something called Operation Metro Surge—shot and killed Renée Good, a woman who had been acting legally as an observer of immigration enforcement activities. A few weeks later they also shot and killed Alex Pretti, who had been protesting. In fact, a Wikipedia page that keeps a tally of immigration shootings during the second Trump Administration counts dozens of shootings by ICE and CBP agents across the country.[2] Journalists and civil rights activists have registered alarm at how immigration enforcement agencies and the National Guard were transforming into a military police force, charged with doing the bidding of the president.[3] Federal Judge Joseph R. Goodwin wrote that "antiseptic judicial rhetoric cannot do justice to what is happening. Across the interior of the United States, agents of the federal government—masked, armed with military weapons, operating from unmarked vehicles, acting without warrants of any kind—are seizing persons for civil immigration violations and imprisoning them without any semblance of due process."[4]

Around the same time Good and Pretti were killed, the Corporation for Public Broadcasting ceased operations. Withering attacks from President Trump and his allies, combined with an act of Congress removing its public funding, resulted in the crumbling of one of the pillars of public media and information in the United States.

In Iran, protests erupted against a violent autocratic regime. Although estimates vary widely because of the Iranian state's tight control of media, between three thousand and thirty-five thousand people likely lost their lives. More on Iran in a moment.

Back in the United States, President Trump floated the idea of investigating and charging Jerome Powell, the chair of the Federal Reserve, because the president did not like Powell's policymaking, which is to be independent of the president and political pressures. Later in 2026, at the end of June, the Supreme Court narrowly blocked Trump's firing of another Federal Reserve governor, which was also widely understood to have been motivated by politics. In a

---

[2] "List of Shootings by U.S. Immigration Agents in the Second Trump Administration," Wikipedia, accessed July 16, 2026, https://en.wikipedia.org/wiki/List_of_shootings_by_U.S._immigration_agents_in_the_second_Trump_administration.

[3] Anne Applebaum, "Federal Agents Are Violating the Rights of Americans," *The Atlantic*, January 9, 2026, https://www.theatlantic.com/podcasts/2026/01/autocracy-in-america-ice-and-the-national-guard/685279/.

[4] Joseph R. Goodwin, Anderson Jesus Urquilla-Ramos v. Donald J. Trump, February 19, 2026, https://www.wvsd.uscourts.gov/content/anderson-jesus-urquilla-ramos-v-donald-j-trump-et-al.

similar case, Senator Mark Kelly of Arizona has been persecuted and threatened with demotion of military rank and legal action after joining other lawmakers in a video reminding soldiers of their obligation to refuse unlawful orders.

In an extraordinary breach of election independence and local control, federal agents seized ballots in Fulton County, Georgia, claiming fraud, and President Trump floated the idea of nationalizing elections.

Regarding a sovereign nation, Trump said, "I do believe I'll have the honor of taking Cuba," and, "I think I can do anything I want with it."[5]

Trump shared a photo of himself styled as Jesus—though after backlash he claimed that he thought it depicted himself as a doctor, and he deleted the image.[6]

In Russia, President Vladimir Putin has continued to hold his grip on the country's finances, media, and war machinery.

Secretary of Defense Pete Hegseth, who has begun referring to himself as the secretary of war, spoke at prayer services at the Pentagon. (Hegseth prefers the new, unofficial title because it matches his preferred new, unofficial name for his agency: The Department of War. Short of an act of Congress, however, he remains Secretary of Defense.) At that service in March 2026, Hegseth prayed for "overwhelming violence of action against those who deserve no mercy,"[7] and in a service the next month he quoted scripture he claimed was from the book of Ezekiel, but which more closely resembled dialogue from the film *Pulp Fiction*.[8]

Around the same time, President Trump called Pope Leo XIV "WEAK on crime, and terrible for Foreign Policy," in his trademark idiosyncratic capitalization.[9] The president's remarks about the pope came as the Holy See

---

[5] "'I Do Believe I Will Have the Honor of Taking Cuba': Trump Says," Associated Press, March 16, 2026, https://newsroom.ap.org/editorial-photos-videos/detail?itemid=7eca50186e4b423c969a7922075d7abd&mediatype=video.

[6] Austin Sarat, "What Trump's Post as a Jesus-Like Figure Tells Us About Political Messianism," *The Conversation*, April 30, 2026, https://theconversation.com/what-trumps-post-as-a-jesus-like-figure-tells-us-about-political-messianism-281415.

[7] Tiffany Stanley, "At Pentagon Christian Service, Hegseth Prays for Violence "Against Those Who Deserve No Mercy,"" Associated Press, March 25, 2026, https://apnews.com/article/pete-hegseth-pentagon-christian-worship-service-30db48b6ceb8af5e6172fb3ba2eafaa0.

[8] Richard Luscombe, "Hegseth Channels His Inner Tarantino with Fake Bible Verse from Pulp Fiction," *The Guardian*, April 16, 2026, https://www.theguardian.com/us-news/2026/apr/16/hegseth-pulp-fiction-ezekiel-prayer.

[9] Jordan Freiman, "Trump Calls Pope Leo 'WEAK on Crime, and Terrible for Foreign Policy,'" April 13, 2026, *The Guardian*, https://www.cbsnews.com/news/trump-pope-leo-weak-on-crime-iran-truth-social/.

seemed to criticize the United States' newest war, which had been launched in late February, against Iran. As of this writing in mid-July of 2026, that war is ongoing, despite several ceasefire agreements, and flaring back into open violence. The war has come at a high cost to human life and at the expense of the global economy, which has struggled to adjust to new restrictions on exports of oil through the Strait of Hormuz.

On his Truth Social network, President Trump shared a post mocking Minnesota kindergarteners. The post, which called attention the kindergarteners' religious dress, came from an account called "End Wokeness" and featured a video of kids of Somali descent—a demographic Trump has previously called "garbage."[10]

In the first year of his second term, President Trump is estimated to have made an income of 2.4 billion dollars.[11]

I could go on. If you have made it this far, you probably know the list as well as I do. In the United States and around the world, autocracy and authoritarianism are having their day. The news cycles only seem to be getting more intense, scarier, and more frantic. Against that backdrop, an ancient text like the Book of Acts might seem quaint or irrelevant. After all, there are plenty of crises in our day and time to keep us busy.

In the time since I submitted the main part of this manuscript, I have become even more convinced that the Book of Acts contains lessons and guidance for us as we navigate these difficult times. By the time you hold this book in your hands, I imagine that even more events will have unfolded that make the story found in the Book of Acts newly relevant to our lives: new acts of state violence, new expressions of xenophobia, new corruption, and new territorial expansion and resource grabs. Even more news cycles will have come and gone, with new outrages and new crises and new causes for fear and despair. I hope I am wrong about that, but I doubt that I am. When those events unfold—when autocrats flex their muscles and leaders enrich and aggrandize themselves and when governments deploy authoritarian tactics to suppress the rights of everyday people—I hope you will be able to return to the Book of Acts, recognize the patterns, and discover anew the power of resistance.

July 20, 2026

---

[10] Erica L. Green and Dylan Freedman, "Trump's Post on Singing Somali Schoolchildren Stir[s] Anger in Minnesota," July 11, 2026, *New York Times*, https://www.nytimes.com/2026/07/11/us/politics/trump-somali-kindergartners.html?smid=nytcore-ios-share.

[11] Dan Alexander, "Trump is Making Three Times as Much in the White House as He Did in Business," *Forbes*, July 15, 2026, https://www.forbes.com/sites/danalexander/2026/07/15/trump-is-making-three-times-as-much-in-white-house-as-he-did-in-business/.